CHATHAM IN THE JAZZ AGE

CHATHAM IN THE JAZZ AGE

DEBRA LAWLESS

THE History PRESS

Published by The History Press
Charleston, SC 29403
www.historypress.net

First published 2009

Manufactured in the United States

ISBN 978.1.59629.620.6

Library of Congress Cataloging-in-Publication Data

Lawless, Debra.
Chatham in the jazz age / Debra Lawless.
p. cm.
Includes bibliographical references.
ISBN 978-1-59629-620-6
1. Chatham (Mass.)--History--20th century. 2. Chatham (Mass.)--Social conditions--20th century. 3. Chatham (Mass.)--Biography. 4. Social change--Massachusetts--Chatham--History--20th century. 5. Community life--Massachusetts--Chatham--History--20th century. I. Title.
F74.C43L39 2009
974.4'92--dc22
2009019597

For John

CONTENTS

AUTHOR'S NOTE

I have tried to examine how certain prominent writers, artists and civic boosters successfully sold the idea of Chatham as a quaint, picturesque village in the period between the town's 1912 bicentennial and the start of the Second World War—and in so doing, changed the town forever. Many of the people whom I use to tell my story were born in the latter quarter of the nineteenth century and came to the modern technologies of electricity and automobiles only after they were adults. I wanted to see life through the eyes of this generation as it coped with the enormous changes and challenges brought by the Great War, medical care before antibiotics, a growing youth culture, increased freedom for women, the Great Depression and, finally, the beginning of the Second World War.

ACKNOWLEDGEMENTS

I would like to thank Ted Whittaker and his cousin Judith Llewellyn for talking to me about the lives of their grandparents, Edwin and Bess Kidder, and for sharing many beautiful family photographs; Mary Ann Gray, archivist at the Chatham, Massachusetts Historical Society, for giving me the germ of the idea that turned into this book and patiently assisting me along the way; George F. Wight, grandson of Alice Stallknecht Wight, for sending me his grandmother's unpublished memoir, *Something of My Past*; Reggie Nickerson for his entertaining tour of Alice Stallknecht's murals, in which he is a subject; Isabel Lamberg for her New Year's Eve eggnog and for her vivid recollections of painting classes with her neighbor Harold C. Dunbar; Priscilla Dalrymple for sharing her knowledge of Joseph C. Lincoln; Marilyn Brown for many discussions of Heman A. Harding; Robert S. Hardy for his recollections of growing up in Chatham; Dwight and Florine Myer for help with paintings and historical photographs at the Chatham Historical Society; Amy Andreasson, reference librarian at the Eldredge Public Library, Chatham, for leads and research help, as well as access to the prototype of the digitized *Chatham Monitor*; Geraldine D. Nickerson for her encouragement and for sharing her late husband Joe's photographs; Don Aikman of the Chatham Historical Commission for allowing me access to the commission's documents of the 1920s and '30s; the Reverend David Erickson and church historian Edward C. Everett of the First Congregational Church of Chatham for graciously allowing me to comb through the church archives; and Norman and Don St. Pierre for insightful discussions of Slim Hutchings, whose gas station they now own. I owe a debt of gratitude to the Chatham Historical Society, which provided much of the archival materials and photographs that make up this book. I also thank my friends at the *Cape Cod Chronicle* for their support.

On a personal level, I would like to thank my husband, John, for his unending forbearance and for reading several drafts; my friend Stuart G. Stearns for early on encouraging me with this project and patiently reading through several drafts; and my friends Jack Collins, Mary Siqueiros, Kathrine Lovell, Christina Plattner Evola and Jo-Anne Sliva and my cousin Barbara Pierce for those "rah rah" telephone calls and e-mails that kept me going.

I would also like to thank my father, Leroy Aaronson; my mother, Barbara Aaronson, died three weeks before I completed this book.

Finally, I thank Saunders Robinson of The History Press for believing in this project and for her careful editing suggestions.

INTRODUCTION

The Cape is all things to all visitors," a 1936 article in the *New York Times* proclaimed. "If one likes the sea and things that are old—little old houses and little old towns—sunset lakes and lily ponds, one will surely like the Cape."

Let us imagine Chatham—the elbow of what Henry David Thoreau called "the bared and bended arm" that is Cape Cod.[1]

These are the waters the Pilgrims on the *Mayflower* sailed into in 1620, only to turn back when they encountered the treacherous shoals and breakers of Pollock Rip. Chatham's wicked coastline is the stuff of legends. The hulls of many rotting ships still lie hidden in the shoals, rips and currents of the elbow.

During the nineteenth century, lighthouses were erected at Monomoy Point, at Stage Harbor and at the edge of Chatham's "Old Village" to increase the odds of mariners looking for a safe passage through Chatham's waters. At the turn of the twentieth century, Chatham was well known for its landmark Twin Lights, the second pair of which had already crumbled into the eroding cliff, eaten away by the swirling Atlantic tides. Visitors and townspeople alike enjoyed sitting with the Twin Lights behind them, drowsily contemplating the dangerous waters where, in those days before the Cape Cod Canal opened, the sails of many ships still dotted the horizon as they rounded the Cape. In a single day, Josiah Hardy, who kept the Chatham Light from 1872 to 1900, counted 365 ships off Chatham—16,000 in the year 1875 alone.

Throughout the seventeenth, eighteenth and nineteenth centuries, the people of this small village made their living from the sea. Some sailed on the great clipper ships, perhaps to find riches in foreign ports; others headed out to the Grand Banks to catch mackerel and cod. The town's fortunes rose and fell with the tides. Most everyone in the treeless, wind-swept town lived off the sea one way or another. Some farmed, some cultivated cranberries

A postcard shows the old Twin Lights erected in 1877. In 1923, the north twin was removed to Nauset. How it was moved is one of the greatest mysteries of Cape Cod. *Photo courtesy of the Chatham, Massachusetts Historical Society.*

and some ran general stores. Due to quirks of geography, industrialization and its immigrant workers largely bypassed the Cape, and by the turn of the twentieth century Chatham's scanty population sagged as young people looked elsewhere for jobs. The town offered little in the way of recreation for visitors, although a few hotels had sprung up for those who cared to venture here on the train to take in the two months of "the season."

By 1916 something new was afoot. Chatham was "the fastest growing town on the Cape, and a very typical one," the *Handbook of New England* proclaimed in 1916.[2] The automobile was on the rise, but so were roads, financed by the commonwealth. The state road from Chatham "was built four or five years ago of Socony asphalt binder and the local sand," and under the dual pressures of sunlight and traffic, "it has formed a smooth roadway."

"'Capers' are proud of the Cape, its low rolling hills, its pine groves, its little lakes, its surf-bordered beaches, its white-painted or gray-shingled houses, its sturdy, law-abiding, dryly witty people," Chatham's famous novelist Joseph C. Lincoln wrote in 1935.[3] Cape Codders were thought to be blunt and honest and somehow to live more authentic—if less fashionable and more primitive—lives than their counterparts in the cities.

But did the "old salt" living the simple life on Cape Cod truly ever exist? Or was he a figment of the imagination of Joseph Lincoln and others who lined their pockets by promoting the myth? Did the sleepy and picturesque Cape ever exist?

"Regions are artifacts of the imagination as well as geographic and cultural entities," scholar Joseph A. Conforti writes.[4] Cape Cod, unlike many other more accessible parts of rural New England, did not develop and sell itself to tourists during the nineteenth century, but its time was at hand in the early twentieth century. While reasons for its late development may be complex, one thing, as scholar Dona Brown points out, remains clear: "Beaches alone do not make a resort. Nature alone does not make 'scenery,' and picturesque history alone does not make a quaint tourist destination…Tourist industries were built by people."[5]

This book will take a look at some of the people—Chatham's native son and preeminent civic booster Heman Andrew Harding; Cape Cod's "yarn spinner" Joseph C. Lincoln; artist and writer Harold C. Dunbar; and muralist Alice Stallknecht Wight—who each, in his or her own way, squarely placed picturesque old Chatham on the national map between 1912 and 1940 and in so doing drew many, many visitors to the town.

Heman Andrew Harding was a Chatham native with a pedigree that stretched back almost to the town's beginnings. Harding's father, Andrew, ran a general store in the part of town later named "the Old Village," near the Twin Lights. Harding, though, chose a different career. After graduating from Harvard Law, he dabbled in local politics and, through his law practice, had his finger in just about every game in town. He was also a great joiner in civic causes and was a moving force behind the town's electrification, the town's water lines and, most significantly, the town's publicity campaign through new groups such as the Chatham Board of Trade and the Cape Cod Chamber of Commerce.

Although Harding was a father of one, the town of Chatham was tantamount to his second child. "He may well be placed in the category of a leading citizen," a directory of the time said.[6] Harding filled his days with legal work and his evenings with meetings; he chaired town committees that eventually built a new high school and town office building. Only occasional ill health seemed to stop Harding from accomplishing more.

The novelist Joseph C. Lincoln was a native of Brewster, about ten miles from Chatham, but in 1915 he built a magnificent summer home, Crosstrees, overlooking the Atlantic in Chatham. In 1900, at the age of thirty, Lincoln had "penciled" his first book about Cape Cod. Since then, every year for the next forty years, he penciled another. His books sold between 30 and

100,000 copies each, his son Freeman Lincoln wrote.[7] Lincoln was often dubbed "the writer who invented Cape Cod."

The dust jacket of Lincoln's Great War novel *Shavings* shows quintessential Cape Cod elements such as a quaint shingled house tucked behind a white picket fence. Pink hollyhocks and blue larkspur grow in profusion. In the distance, a sail can be seen on the blue sea. Yet did such a house, and the simple, virtuous life it suggested, exist outside of Lincoln's imagination and those who produced picture postcards?

While elsewhere in New England residents dealt with industrialization and hordes of immigrants, on Joseph Lincoln's Cape Cod no such things existed. Because Cape Cod was, essentially, an economic backwater with a homogenous white population, Lincoln was able to choose details to create a kind of fictional Eden. "Consumers found the mythical cape very attractive and locals specialized in selling them what they sought," Lincoln scholar William D. Moore has asserted.[8]

Living not far from Joseph Lincoln's summer house, Crosstrees, within hearing but not sight of the Atlantic, was the American impressionist painter Harold Dunbar. Dunbar, who grew up in Brockton in the shadows of the shoe factories, came to Chatham in 1915 and almost immediately began manufacturing a vision of the Cape that coincided with Lincoln's. First through his paintings of iconic scenes, such as the Old Mill set on a hillside above a pond, and then through newspaper and magazine articles that extolled the virtues of Chatham as a place untouched by crime and other urban blights, Dunbar also lured more tourists to town.

In December 1922, Dunbar painted a cover for *Cape Cod Magazine*. Called *Snow Scene on the Mill Pond at Chatham*, the painting is revealing in the way that Dunbar carefully manipulated actual architectural and natural elements to create a fictional scene. With the horizon roughly midway up the canvas, four silver poplars give the painting an upward thrust. The Methodist Episcopal church, with its characteristic four-pronged steeple and clock, sits off-center, almost on the sandy beach of the Mill Pond rather than on Main Street. In the foreground are two quaint Cape houses with shuttered windows, each with an outbuilding. Two children with a sled are rolling a giant ball of snow. All is tranquil, safe and mightily appealing—a classic image of Cape Cod or New England. Yet the title, *Snow Scene on the Mill Pond at Chatham*, tells the viewer that the painting depicts an actual place in an actual town.

In 1910, Alice Stallknecht Wight, a painter trained in New York City, and her husband, Carol Wight, established themselves on a derelict farm

"He was short, fat, laughing, and infinitely friendly," novelist Joseph C. Lincoln's son Freeman wrote about his father. "He loved Cape Cod, people, and good food." Lincoln wrote more than forty novels and plays set on Cape Cod. *Photo courtesy of the Chatham, Massachusetts Historical Society.*

at the end of Stage Harbor Road. In the '30s, Alice Stallknecht entered an extraordinary period of artistic creativity. Taking as her subject the townspeople, she painted them in three murals that one contemporary artist has described in style as a cross between Norman Rockwell and Edvard Munch.[9] Her first mural, *Christ Preaching to the Multitude*, mounted inside the front doors of the Congregational Church, was featured in *Time* magazine in 1932; Stallknecht became famous and so did her subjects. Although some thought the paintings, which used a Chatham gas station owner as the model for Christ, blasphemous, thousands traipsed through the church each summer for a look.

Although Stallknecht's vision of Chatham in the 1930s is harsher than Dunbar's, it also serves to counter the alienation often found in modern urban life. Stallknecht's models are all white, reinforcing the idea of Chatham's homogenous population. (They are, in many cases, related to one another and show family similarities.) And they are engaged in some form of religious practice—listening to Christ preaching from a dory or sitting down to a church supper. Again, iconic elements of Chatham appear in the mural: the lighthouse atop its bluff, a dory and men wearing uniforms of the U.S. Coast Guard.

Chatham, with its tight family circles, was not, as Alice Stallknecht later wrote, an easy town in which to assimilate. In 1912, one-quarter of the marriages in town were contracted between Chatham residents, and only one-fifth involved one party from off-Cape.

The world beyond Chatham had changed a great deal in recent decades, and so, during the Great War, would Chatham. When Lincoln, Dunbar and Stallknecht arrived in Chatham, most townspeople had no reason to see their futures as differing significantly from those of their parents. (Harding, who had been educated in the Boston area, was an exception.) Yet partly because of the town's strategic position on the coast, world events intruded. In 1914, Guglielmo Marconi built a wireless station in Chatham; that station was crucial to military communications during both world wars. During the Great War, the U.S. Navy established an air station on Nickerson's Neck overlooking Pleasant Bay, bringing many strangers to town. While summer tourism seemed to be the answer to the economic blight that marked Cape Cod, residents also learned that prosperity brought its own problems. Automobiles created traffic snarls and crime increased. Life just wasn't so peaceful anymore.

To what extent Harding, Lincoln, Dunbar and Stallknecht were conscious boosters of Chatham is ultimately unknowable, yet each contributed mightily to the popularization of Chatham as the epitome of classic Cape Cod.

The daughters of Chatham selectman Edwin Kidder, Ann Elizabeth Kidder Whittaker (left) and Emma "Kathleen" Kidder, fish at Monomoy during the summer of 1937. The Kidders, who came to town in 1914, were in the vanguard of Chatham's summer colony. *Photo courtesy of Ted Whittaker.*

"Ask a New Yorker why he likes the Cape and he tells you it is 'different.' Sometimes he says it is 'quaint,'" the 1936 *New York Times* article tells us.

Quaint, when cleverly coupled with modern amenities, would prove a tough combination to beat.

THE END OF RAGTIME

Home Sweet Home

Mid pleasures and palaces though I may roam,
Be it ever so humble, there's no place like home;
A charm from the sky seems to hallow us there,
Which, seek thro' the world, is ne'er met with elsewhere. Home.

—Nineteenth-century folk song by Henry Bishop

In 1916, the terrain around Chatham's Twin Lights was a mess. Three or four garden seats were plunked down in "rough and uncared for" ground so that visitors could sit for a moment to admire the dramatic view of ships passing through the dangerous shoals of the Atlantic off Chatham.

In an August 8, 1916 letter that may have exaggerated the numbers but nevertheless suggested the site's future popularity, Heman Andrew Harding, a prominent Cape Cod lawyer and resident of Chatham, wrote:

> *Our own people frequent it a great deal and thousands of people residing or stopping in other parts of the Cape, and residents of states all through the Union, come there each year, stop, get out of their cars, and spend considerable time looking off.*

Harding was writing to Congressman Joseph Walsh in Washington, D.C., asking permission to beautify and tame the site, which came under federal jurisdiction as a part of the lighthouses' grounds.[10]

Why do lighthouses attract? Is it because, usually set on bluffs overlooking treacherous stretches of sea, they invite the mind to contemplate invincible mariners fighting one on one with the primeval sea? Or is it because lighthouses and their keepers perform their duties in the loneliness of the night, beckoning to those in peril on the waters?

Adding to the drama of the Twin Lights site, the picturesque ruins of the old brick lighthouses that fell into the sea in 1881 were still crumbling in the eroding bluff below the current lights. Down below that, crashing up against the beach, were the waters of the wicked shoals, rips and currents of the Atlantic, just about a mile above the elbow of the arm that is the Cape. The hearty souls on the *Mayflower*, wandering into this spot due to an error in navigation, had turned back to Provincetown. Later, high above on the bluff, tenderly watching over those foolish or brave enough to sail through here, stood Chatham's Twin Lights, fixed beams that saved many a ship from ruin.

Yes, people who came here knew all of this, or felt it, and they were powerfully drawn to the site. Yet for the many who flocked to this spot, "there are no accommodations."

So why not, practical Harding asks, beautify the area? Erect a few concrete markers "of historic and romantic interest," calling attention to the "historic and other interests of the shore and the water in that locality"? Why not put up a six-to-eight-foot-diameter "dial with arrows pointing to points of public interest"? How about a few shrubs, plants, vines and even a pagoda with a seat inside "as a bit of shelter from the sun"?

And why not point out to tourists something of the history of the spot—explain to them that the Massachusetts Humane Society once maintained "huts of refuge" along the shore for those poor souls rescued from ships going down in this famously treacherous spot.

Walsh approved Harding's ideas, and the strip along the lighthouse was leased to the town under a revocable lease in 1916.

Harding's ideas represent an early conscious attempt to market Chatham as a tourist attraction rather than as a working fishing village. In the early twentieth century, Cape Cod, unlike much of the rest of New England, including its coastline from Maine to Rhode Island, was an unexplored tourist area.[11] In the 1920s, the automobile and improved roads alone would not turn Chatham and the rest of the Cape into the tourist mecca they are today. Another element was needed—clever marketing of the Cape's fast-disappearing "quaint" past, whether real or imagined. Today, the Chatham Lighthouse (its twin was moved to Nauset in 1923) is perhaps the most visited spot in Chatham. Harding was a man with a vision of the future.

Born on February 6, 1871, Harding graduated from Chatham High school at age sixteen. After several years working at painting, fishing and clerking at a Chatham hotel to earn money for his education, he entered Harvard College as a freshman at the age of twenty-one. He followed that with a law degree from Harvard in 1898 and then for a time managed the Mattaquason.

As a child, they called him Andy. Andy was the only child of Andrew Harding, proprietor of the general store that sold bootlaces, shovels, harnesses, dill pickles and candy. "It don't seem natural to call you anything else," a childhood friend wrote many years later, upon Andrew's death, when Heman was one of Chatham's most eminent men.

Sometimes a self-made man doesn't want to be reminded of his humble roots. But Heman A. Harding, as he chose to be known later in life, could not have minded since he chose to live out his days in the town where he was born and where his ancestors set down roots as early as 1690.

While an undergraduate at Harvard in 1891, he began to keep records of expenses in a leather-bound notebook. Typical expenses were carfare, a German grammar and a Latin lexicon, tuition (fifty-five dollars), a twenty-five-cent haircut and fifteen cents of washing. His bookkeeping was fastidious—a harbinger of the organized lawyer he was to become. "Mistake somewhere but all my bills are straight," he wrote on one page marked by many erasures, and on the next, "I have a 3-cent piece in my pocket. This may have made the trouble."[12]

After Harvard Law School, and when he had already served as selectman and school committeeman, he became engaged to a local girl, Edith Crowell Farmer, whose parents ran the Monomoyick Inn on Main Street. Harding and Farmer must have known each other most of their lives, but they took their time settling down. By the time of their wedding, he was thirty-six; she was four years younger.

They married on Valentine's Day 1907, and from his letters it is easy to believe that the sentimental date was chosen as much by him as by her.

An unknown wit wrote a poem about Harding that was apparently presented to the "After Dinner Club, Barnstable," in January 1908, a few months after the Hardings' wedding. In rhyme, the poet speaks of observing the burly, 223-pound Harding missing a train, spending the day at home "with wifey," engaged in domestic activities, and resolving to get up earlier the next morning. The Hardings' only child, Virginia Avis Harding, was born nine months later, in October 1908. "Girl born this morning Edith in best condition sends love Heman A. Harding," Harding wrote in a telegram that afternoon.

During a trip to New York on business for the Board of Harbor and Land Commissioners, Heman wrote to Edith, "It is drawing toward dark now, and I do wish I were going home to my dear wife and child. I am actually homesick. I love my wife and my child deeply and miss them both sorely." He

Town luminaries Edith and Heman, with their daughter Virginia Harding, 1933. The trio had their fingers in politics and civic and club matters. "Now there's a 'prissy-puss,'" Virginia wrote on the back of the photo. "Why did I look so smug?" *Photo courtesy of the Chatham, Massachusetts Historical Society.*

signed the letter "Your Loving Husband and Father Heman A. Harding," adding his characteristic flourish to the double *H*s, with the *A* nestled in between. Virginia signed her childhood cards to her father as "Ginger" and "the littlest bear."

"Dad was a most devoted husband and father and would never go anywhere unless Mother and I could go too," Virginia recalled after his death.

In 1913, Harding bought stately Prospect House on Main Street, which he entirely renovated before Edith and Virginia moved in. His Chatham law office was just down the street, and his Barnstable office was adjacent to the courthouse on Route 6A. While practicing law, Harding rose quickly in Chatham politics, beginning with the school board, moving on to the selectmen and then jumping up to wider Cape Cod politics.

Barely any activity of any significance occurred in town that Harding didn't have his finger in. The Marconi Company wanted to set up a radio station in Chatham? Harding was the man to see about untangling the deeds and acquiring the land. Townspeople wanted to electrify Chatham? Harding sat on the committee, and eventually his house became the first private home

The Marconi Corporation established a radio station here in 1915. During World War I, the station was taken over by the federal government, and later by RCA, bringing many outsiders to Chatham. Plans are now afoot for a radio museum. *Photo by the author.*

to be electrified. Need to raise money for Liberty Bonds? Harding raised 15 percent above the quota. At the annual town meeting held in February of each year, Harding could be counted on to comment on almost every warrant on the article.

At the age of forty-one, Harding, who had an intense interest in local history, was one of the movers and shakers behind the 1912 bicentennial celebration.

William Smith's *History*

Interest in the town's two-hundred-year history had been growing in the new century. In 1909, Heman Harding's decade-older friend and colleague at the bar, Selectman William C. Smith, published the first volume of what would be a four-volume *History of Chatham, Massachusetts*. The second volume appeared in 1913, just after the bicentennial.

Smith labored under tremendous handicaps while writing his *History*. "Few, if any, of the towns in the State have been more unfortunate than

Chatham in respect to the preservation of historical materials," he wrote in his preface.[13] In 1827, a fire in the Barnstable County Courthouse destroyed records pertaining to Chatham. In 1861, the parsonage of Chatham's First Congregational Church burned down while Pastor Edward B. French and his wife were attending a prayer meeting. (Friends collected $700 for the Frenches to start over again, but the records could never be replaced.) And in 1919, two years after the third volume of Smith's *History* was published, Chatham Town Hall burned down, apparently from a carelessly tossed cigarette. Fortunately, Smith had already incorporated many of the town hall records into his *History*, thus preserving them.

Another cloud under which Smith labored, not mentioned in the book's preface, was his ill health. In a memorial article published after Smith's death, Harding noted that Smith continued his work despite "the serious handicap of an injury to his foot which has given him much trouble all through his life and may well have been the cause of much of the illness from which he has suffered." By Harding's tabulations, Smith had been ill during thirty-two of the previous forty years.

At the time of the bicentennial, William Smith was fifty years old. He was born in Chatham, and as a child in 1865 he had spent time at sea, sailing home from Cadiz and Malaga, Spain, with his parents and his brother, Lucas, who kept a diary of the voyage. After graduating from Chatham High at age sixteen, William attended Phillips Exeter Academy and then earned his bachelor's degree at Harvard, graduating second in a class of two hundred. After that came Harvard Law.

Smith's first job out of Harvard Law was at the newspaper the *State* in Lowell, where he early on displayed his love of writing and ferreting out facts. By 1889, he was practicing law in Boston at the law offices of Robert Stone; he then moved to the offices of Heman Chaplin and James R. Caret. In Caret's office, he investigated titles and got acquainted with the old Supreme Court of Judicature files, from which he drew many important contributions to his historical work, according to Harding. From 1885 to 1898, in addition to practicing law, he contributed many articles to *Appleton's Encyclopedia*.

Back in Chatham, Smith trod much the same route through local politics as Harding, serving on the school committee and board of selectmen. Disappointingly, no doubt, in 1918 another ambitious Chatham man, Erastus T. Bearse, who was Smith's near contemporary, crushed Smith in a Republican primary election for the Second Barnstable Representative District. Smith "served the Town with ability and fidelity," Harding wrote about Smith.[14] "Even as a youth, he sought out local material for a history of

Chatham, discovering a wealth of most important information which, but for his work, might well have been lost."

Calling Smith's *History of Chatham, Massachusetts* a "masterpiece," Harding added that it was "built like a law-book with its extensive and accurate footnotes on history and genealogy." He called it an authoritative "source of enjoyment, information and pride to all who love Chatham."

To pay for the publication, Smith sold subscriptions. Harding took one, as did the painter Harold Dunbar, a summer resident who led plein-air painting classes. Carol Van Buren Wight, another newcomer to town, signed up for one subscription and then signed up his wife Alice Stallknecht Wight's Champlain Tea Room for an additional three. Later, Wight committed himself to five more copies. Local businesses, including the ice cream shop Quilty's and the variety shop the Mayflower, subscribed to the book, as did Goodspeed's Bookstore in Boston, libraries and historical societies, bringing the subscription list to 372 copies.[15]

Although the official bicentennial anniversary of the town's founding fell on June 12, town officials graciously rescheduled the two-day hoopla to the first days of August so that a maximum number could participate after the official "season" began on the Fourth of July. A postcard invitation to the event featured a photograph of Chatham's iconic site—the Twin Lights, with the Mack monument commemorating the 1902 sinking of the barge *Wadena* next to them. "The attendance strained the town's accommodations," a reporter wrote in the *Barnstable Patriot* the week after the celebration.

Despite the enthusiasm of many townspeople, town officials hadn't given much thought to the bicentennial until a few months beforehand. (The town's centennial had passed unremarked during the War of 1812.) During a February 8, 1911 meeting, townspeople voted to appoint a committee of three "to retire and bring in a list of fifteen named persons to serve on a committee for the celebration of the two hundredth anniversary of the incorporation of the town of Chatham in the year 1912."[16] The following year, townspeople allocated $750 of town money to go toward the gala, and the committees got to work.

On August 1, 1912, "the weather of the first morning was of the most discouraging aspect," the official published report of the bicentennial noted.[17] "The rain came down in torrents and seemingly would disarrange all plans for the day." After the parade was postponed due to initially inclement weather, townsfolk gathered at the town's whimsical Gothic railroad station to meet invited guests. Governor Eugene Noble Foss was expected but didn't appear, as he was detained in Boston by state business. A line formed behind the deputy sheriffs to head into town. First came a light-keeping marshal and his staff of rough riders, then the twenty-one-piece Salem Cadet Band, a line of horse-drawn carriages with invited guests, speakers and town officials and, finally, a line of summer residents in their motor cars, a hint of the modern era to come.

In 1912, the automobile had been on the road for barely a decade. The horse and carriage were still the common mode of transportation. Local roads were mainly dirt, with the better roads having a slick of tar over the sand to provide a reasonably firm surface. Yet a contingent of summer folk sat in their cars, rolling along at the end of the procession. Twenty-seven "non-native" summer residents with names like Pennypacker, Wentworth, Loveland, Shattuck and Horton are recorded as donating $309 toward the festivities. Another group of twelve "native" summer residents donated an additional $216.

In his bicentennial speech, the Honorable James W. Hawes, a Chatham native then living in New York City, touched on the presence of summer folk by quoting a 1791 writer: "The winds in every direction come from the sea, and invalids by visiting the Cape sometimes experience the same benefit as from going to sea." Already in 1912, 29 percent of the town's real estate taxes were paid by nonresidents.

The sun broke through the clouds by nine thirty that morning, and skies remained clear as six hundred sat down to dinner under a circus tent at a property on Cross Street then called the Rockwell grounds, today's Chase Park. During the heavy midday banquet, Smith, who served on two committees—he chaired the Historic Sites committee and also served on the committee for the Reception of Invited Guests—shared a table with seventeen other dignitaries, including Joseph C. Lincoln and the Reverend Samuel H. Emery, who gave the invocation. You might think that fish would have featured prominently in the grand banquet of this town that made its living from the sea, but in fact no fish appeared on a menu that included cold roast turkey, boiled ham and boiled tongue.

After dinner, served from an outdoor kitchen by pretty local girls ages fourteen to eighteen dressed in white, the group sang "Home Sweet Home." One can imagine six hundred voices in the open air raised in song, accompanied by the Salem Cadet Band. Perhaps a few cried during the treacly song, which must have had particular meaning both to those who had never left town and to those who had made good in the wider world and returned for the historic occasion.

If fish didn't feature on the gala menu, those making speeches after the meal nodded to the town's raison d'être. In his opening speech, C.A. Freeman told the crowd:

We pay our grateful homage and raise our voices in thanksgiving and praise to yonder booming ocean, which, as our constant companion, through the centuries, has also been equally constant in its never failing resources, ever bountiful of its stores for our comfort and profit.

Joshua Atkins Nickerson II, then eleven years old, was hawking commemorative badges and souvenirs from a large basket on his arm. In his 1988 memoir *Days to Remember*, Nickerson clocks the after-dinner speeches at a stupefying two hours.[18]

The longest address was delivered by James Hawes, Smith's uncle, a native son who had moved to New York City. (In its printed version, Hawes's speech reached an astonishing 47 pages in the 119-page commemorative book.) Hawes, relying on Smith's research, recapped Chatham's early history beginning with the arrival of Europeans.

A Few Hardy Souls

The town was originally known as Monomoyick, named after the Indian tribe prevalent in these parts. In October 1606, when Samuel de Champlain and his party arrived, they famously skirmished with the initially friendly Indians at the place later known as Port Fortune. Champlain, who was a French cartographer, left valuable maps to posterity.

In 1603 or 1604, William Nickerson, destined to become the father of Chatham, was born in England. A weaver by trade, Nickerson set sail from England to avoid religious persecution on April 15, 1637. He arrived on June 20 in Salem and, after living in Yarmouth for a few years, bought land from Mattaquason, sachem of Monomoit, in 1656. But Nickerson failed to gain the consent of the colonial authorities for his real estate transaction and so entered into lengthy wrangling with the Crown, finally settling the matter in 1672 for ninety pounds.

When Nickerson first arrived in Chatham, "forests of huge oaks and pines adorned the hills now bare and infertile, while the swamps, now cleared for the cranberry, were almost impenetrable thickets, out of which rose a rich growth of towering cedar." Settlers soon managed to deforest most of the pine, oak and cedar trees to feed their need for housing logs and fuel. Early on, erosion caused by the fierce ocean winds became a concern. Nickerson built his family home near the head of Ryder's Cove—a spot that current Nickersons believe they have accurately marked. For the next twenty-five years, the Nickersons settled down to farming and shellfishing,

In 1915, descendants of William Nickerson, the founder of Chatham, set up a grave plaque in a small cemetery off A. Leonard Way, the probable burial place of the early Nickerson family. *Photo by the author.*

and Chatham was "but little more than a Nickerson neighborhood," Smith tells us.

Smith's *History* tells the story of a small band of hardy souls who persevered against extreme hardship to thrive. They fought the climate and disease, but they were for the most part fortunate as Smith does not record violence between the settlers and the local Indians. As Smith told a gathering of the Smith clan a few years later, "Your ancestors maintained a dignity and an almost absolute universal chastity. They were stern and unrelenting in their morals, God fearing and Sabbath observing people."

The early years were tough, with William Nickerson himself acting as minister. The town financed the Congregational church until about 1759, when the voices of Quakers and Baptists protesting their tax money bankrolling the Congregationalists were finally heard. In 1700, the group voted to build a "meten house" and did so in a now out-of-the-way area off Old Queen Anne Road. Their first minister was a Mr. Vickery, who drowned with several others after the boat they were riding in capsized on April 30, 1702.

In 1711, one year before the town incorporated, "the outlook to many of the villagers seemed so dark that, in the spring and summer of 1711, thirteen families emigrated from the village for one reason or another," Smith writes. This departure became known as "the first emigration," which left thirty-three families in town. Three additional "emigrations" occurred in 1740, 1760 and 1800.

In 1765, five years after the "third emigration," a smallpox epidemic broke out. Townsfolk had coped previously with isolated cases among soldiers or sailors returning from the West Indies, but they had no experience with an epidemic. According to Smith, the 1765 epidemic was said to have originated in the family of Deacon Paul Crowell. How he had contracted the disease is unknown, although one theory said that the disease came from a package of clothing from the West Indies that someone had washed in Crowell's house. Another theory said that the disease came from a bale of Southern cotton on sale at a store near the home of Reuben Ryder.

Smallpox had broken out periodically since the colonials first arrived in the New World. From 1616 to 1619, smallpox killed almost nine-tenths of the Indian population in the Massachusetts Bay area, and Boston residents were victims of regular outbreaks, thanks mainly to the disease arriving with sailors on incoming ships.

The incubation period after exposure ran from twelve to fourteen days, after which a person suffered from a high fever, malaise and head and body aches. The rash began with small red spots on the tongue and mouth and, after a few days, turned into raised bumps filled with a thick, opaque fluid. Pustules formed. When the scabs fell off, they left marks on the skin that eventually became pitted scars. Death occurred in 30 percent of all cases. Some were left blind.[19]

In Chatham between late November 1765 and January 1766, sixty-one persons were infected, with thirty-seven of those dying. "Schools were closed, business abandoned, and the community generally was in a state of fear and consternation. Whole families were almost wiped out." The Ryder family alone lost seventeen members. As was common in situations with contagious epidemics, funeral services were omitted, with bodies rapidly buried in the rear of their respective farms. Crumbling gray stones in the smallpox cemetery tucked in the woods off today's Old Comers Road are a mute and sad testament to the lives lost. The town's first doctor, Samuel Lord, died on January 12, 1766, while ministering to the victims. He is buried in a solitary grave by the side of Training Field Road.

While writing his *History*, Smith visited as many of the sites as possible, including the Smith burial place, near Training Field Road. "If there is a more attractive and picturesque spot on Cape Cod than this location, I have never discovered it," he told a gathering of the Smith clan in the 1920s. "I know this section as intimately as the squirrel or the wood chuck and it is a capital place to go when nature is at its best."

By the time of the 1790 census, the population of the town was 1,140, with 193 families, 20 of which were Nickerson households and 26 of which were Eldredges. Since 1740, most men had been making their living on the sea fishing for cod. Farming was left to boys and older men who raised corn, rye, wheat, flax and tobacco. They drew hay from the salt marshes and, up until the Civil War, raised cattle and sheep. Along the shore, they dug clams, quahogs and oysters. The waters had abundant lobsters, and the woods provided beach plums, wild grapes and cranberries.

The town had no doctor, with residents depending on "matrons of the village with their herb gardens. Later the minister generally had some knowledge of medicine and dentistry," Smith says. The minister was also known to draw up wills and, trained as he was in one of the Ivy League colleges, served as the town's resident intellectual as well.

After finishing his survey of town history, Hawes offered a hint of things to come:

> *It has…only been in comparatively recent years that increasing numbers of summer guests have visited Chatham and found health and pleasure in its salt air and cool breezes and in its wonderful facilities for boating and fishing.*

Within two years, a magnificent seaside inn would be built to take advantage of an oceanfront view and a stretch of white beach. The future was upon them.

Hawes's speech finally wound up on a personal note. "Those who have remained here can scarcely understand our feelings as we visit this scene of our childhood and youth," he said. "Can we ever forget?"

Clearly, this dwindling fishing community of only 1,564 residents—its population had lost 1,200 residents since it peaked in 1860—took fierce pride in itself and its two hundred-year history.

A Turning Point

Although the townspeople didn't know it, the 1912 celebration of Chatham's bicentennial was, in many ways, a swan song service. Soon to be lost was a way of life that had been continuing steadily, with incremental improvements, more or less since William Nickerson arrived in Chatham in 1656. Farming and fishing—the seasons of the land and sea—dictated the rhythms of the town. Coincidentally, the town's oldest resident, Ziba Nickerson, died on August 1, the opening day of the bicentennial, at the age of eighty-eight years and eleven months. Ziba's death no doubt caused a few to nod sagely and reflect that Ziba had held on just long enough to witness the start of the momentous event.

Chatham in 1912 was the kind of town that the writer Joseph C. Lincoln was beginning to make famous through his short stories and novels, beginning with *Cap'n Eri* in 1904. To many off-Cape readers, it was a quaint and picturesque place populated by eccentrics and authentic old salts. Just that year, Lincoln had published *The Postmaster*, "sixteen chapters in which Cap'n Zebulon Snow, Ostable Postmaster, is involved in village life and politics."

By 1912, the town had much of which to boast. Its real estate had topped the $1 million mark the previous year. The school physician, F.B. Worthing, reported that the vast majority of parents were complying with the state's vaccination law, an improvement over the previous year, and that the schools counted only a small number of "actual defectives." Nearly fourteen thousand feet of new oil roads—a thin layer of hot liquid tar or asphalt that was then covered with sand—were planned that year for Chatham Port and South and West Chatham.[20]

The town allocated money every year to a shipwreck fund. In 1912, the town bought railroad tickets to Boston for the crews of the schooners *Kalevala* and *Electric Flash*. The railroad itself had been making it easier for Chatham residents to travel to Boston since the eight-mile spur was extended to Chatham in 1887. Telephone service had been in place since 1883, and before that, starting in 1859, Ziba Nickerson himself had overseen the telegraph.

True, the population had been steadily declining since it hit a high of 2,710 during the Civil War. By 1910, Chatham's numbers had dropped to 1,564—barely the size of a modern high school. The trouble was, fishing was a tough and erratic way to make a living—and there weren't any other games in town.

In 1912, Chatham's technology differed not significantly from that of a century previous. Water was still pumped by hand; it was dark at night, with only kerosene lamps and candles to pierce the inky blackness. Schoolchildren walked to one of nine schools, most of them one-room schoolhouses. The school department had trouble retaining teachers due to salaries that were low even by early twentieth-century standards—$82 a month for a man and $38 for a woman—and the dullness of life for a young person living so far from the gaiety of the city. "The Cape is therefore a sort of a training ground for teachers."[21] Women were still wearing their skirts long and their hair piled atop their heads. Men still buttoned their trousers, as the zipper lay in the future. The off-season, with nothing but the sound of the tides and the icy wind, could prove tedious.

A few months after townspeople decided to host the bicentennial celebration, the White Star's ship *Titanic* sank. Elsewhere in the world in 1912, firsts were being recorded: a man parachuted for the first time from an airplane; an airplane flew the first nonstop flight from Paris to London; and Roald Amundsen reached the South Pole. Ragtime sheet music for the piano would remain popular for a few more years, at least until the Great War ended and a craze for jazz began. Yet without mass communications—the home radio was still a few years off—a mass culture could not yet take hold, and townspeople relied on the *Chatham Monitor*, which began publishing weekly in 1871, for their news.

In 1912, Chatham was still a fishing village, small but proud, with an honorable history of sending many captains and crews to the high seas. Late in the nineteenth century, William E. Nickerson of Cambridge had written some new lyrics to the tune of "Glory, Glory, Hallelujah" that were apt for the bicentennial: "While here upon our native heath our joyous songs we sing, And round about us Chatham hills their echoes backward fling, We'll shout the name of Chatham till earth and sky shall ring, And celebrate this day."

Chatham's Favorite (Adopted) Son

Joseph Lincoln's remarks at the bicentennial celebration, which consisted mainly of three poems, must have followed Hawes's speech as a fluffy dessert follows a heavy meal.

Ironically, the man whom many people nationwide would come to consider Chatham's most famous native son was neither a native son nor a full-time resident of the Cape. Joseph Crosby Lincoln was born in Brewster on February 13, 1870. His father, a sea captain, died on a voyage before the boy was one year old. Lincoln and his widowed mother, Emily, continued to live in Brewster until Lincoln was thirteen, when they moved to Chelsea[22] so Emily could find work as a dress- or hat maker. As a teenager, Lincoln returned to the Cape in the summers, lodging in Chatham with cousins. He had, in fact, spent the earlier part of the summer of 1912 abroad, mainly in England, with side trips to the continent and Switzerland.

Lincoln had originally planned to be an illustrator, but when his writing surpassed his drawing skills, he began publishing an oeuvre that would eventually include over forty novels, plays and essays and earn him a great deal of money. He married Florence Elry Sargent in 1897, and about a year later the pair moved from Chelsea to New York, eventually settling in New Jersey. By the age of forty-six, in 1916, Lincoln was prosperous enough to build a grand house, Crosstrees, on the Boulevard (later Shore Road), with a breathtaking view of the Atlantic Ocean. The house, which stands today, quickly became a favorite subject for postcard photographers and sightseers. "Every summer hundreds of tourists knocked at the door of his Cape Cod summer cottage," his son Freeman wrote.[23] The setting of the house embodied the iconic Cape Cod elements of Lincoln's books, confirming in the tourists' minds that Cape Cod was what Lincoln said it was. Next to the house was a windmill, and in Lincoln's yard "hollyhocks grow in profusion and a colorful old fashioned garden greets visitors," a July 29, 1939 *Monitor* article noted. Lincoln was generally photographed in front of his white picket fence with flowers, the windmill and the blue Atlantic in the background.

The humble yellow pencil with an eraser became Lincoln's trademark—he was said to write his novels and short stories "with plenty of yellow paper and a soft stubby pencil. He will have no typewriter and everything he has published is the result of painstaking work." Newspaper readers of the 1920s and '30s were fascinated by the precise working formula of a successful author and could not read enough about Lincoln's pencil. He was frequently photographed with a pencil, and the title of his biography is *The Prolific Pencil*.

Lincoln enjoyed a sometimes uneasy relationship with the people of Chatham. Although Lincoln brought many, many tourists to Chatham, commentators often note the distaste of townsfolk in seeing themselves, or imagining that they saw themselves, in strange or unflattering fictional settings. Lincoln was said to draw many of his characters from life after eavesdropping on townspeople's conversations in places such as the front porch of Andrew Harding's general store, described as "a rendezvous for all seagoing men of the neighborhood." Later on, when townspeople began to suspect that they saw themselves in Lincoln's books, "the yarning" stopped when the portly Lincoln waddled up. Although Lincoln no doubt incorporated elements of various people into his characters, his people were, ultimately, as fictional as the Cape he set them in.

In the remarks that preceded his poems, Lincoln struck a light, modern tone. After humorously mentioning that he was not a native of Chatham by virtue of his birth in Brewster—"that is not Brewster's fault, of course; so far as I know it is, in other respects, a perfectly respectable community"—Lincoln went on to extol the pleasures of Chatham. "I have basked in the sunshine of your beaches and its warmth has burned into my heart—as well as my neck. Your fish have fed me, and, upon several of my many sailing excursions I have, well, I have returned the compliment." He asserted that the mosquitoes of Monomoy, an eight-mile sandy peninsula that was home to many fishing and gunning camps, loved *him* more than anyone else. "And," he concluded, "I sincerely hope you will invite me to your three hundredth anniversary." Although Lincoln died in March 1944 in Winter Park, Florida, his ashes were transported back to Chatham for burial at Union Cemetery.

"He was short, fat, laughing, and infinitely friendly," Lincoln's only son, Freeman, wrote about his father years after his death.[24] "He loved Cape Cod, people, and good food." Lincoln's characters eat clam fritters, biscuits, fried fish, sea clam pie, codfish tongues, huckleberry dumplings with cream sauce and, for breakfast, apple pie—all solid New England fare.

After Lincoln sat down, William Smith concluded the bicentennial speeches. Smith referred to the "constantly growing summer resort" and almost eerily predicted the rise of history as a marketable tourist commodity:

> *If there is any person in this audience who desires to add some features of abiding interest to this part of the Cape...he could do no better than to erect at suitable points in this town three permanent memorials to these three historic events, the visit of Champlain in 1606, the turning back of the* Mayflower *in 1620 and the death of the saver of Plymouth County* [the Indian Squanto, who died and was presumably buried near Pleasant Bay in 1622].

Alice Stallknecht and Carol Wight

Very likely sitting with his wife on a bench at one of the long tables at the feast, listening to the speeches, was a man who eventually, in 1924, would do just that—erect a memorial to the French explorer Samuel de Champlain across the street from his home on Stage Harbor Road.

Carol Van Buren Wight and his wife, Alice Stallknecht Wight, who would later gain national fame and local notoriety through her Expressionistic murals of townsfolk, were newcomers to town, having arrived just two years earlier after buying a derelict farm from Frank and Grace Mayo. Chatham's history appealed mightily to Carol Wight, who was a Johns Hopkins–trained classicist.

In *Every Man to his Trade*, Alice Stallknecht painted her husband, Carol Wight, next to a monument commemorating Samuel de Champlain's 1606 landing in Chatham. Wight, a professor of classics, was the Chatham Historical Society's historian and was responsible for erecting the monument. *Photo by the author from a painting at the Chatham, Massachusetts Historical Society.*

During the bicentennial, the Wight house, along with the Harding and Smith houses, was one of seventy-eight houses and municipal buildings decorated for the occasion. Carol also, on the second day of festivities, entered a powerboat race on Mill Pond and came in second, just one minute, twenty-eight seconds after the winner, Charles Kendrick, earning five dollars.

The Party Continues

Townspeople celebrating the bicentennial were unusually energetic. After the afternoon's meal and lengthy speeches, they gathered again at the Old Town Hall, which was draped in pink and green and electrified just for the party using some kind of generator. "These lights, never before introduced into the building, were supplied through the efforts of Mr. Charles Lake, manager of the local moving picture entertainments," the commemorative book boasts. People from neighboring towns arrived in cars to walk through a receiving line, shaking hands with thirty-four town dignitaries, including Heman and Edith Harding and William and Florence Smith.

The next morning, the parade, postponed due to rain the previous morning, marched up Main Street to the Rockwell grounds. As was fitting of a salute to the eighteenth and nineteenth centuries, "the parade committee… had decided that automobiles should not be permitted in the parade nor in the prize competition." Still, modern life did intrude:

> *Capt. C.S. Kent drove a replica of the Chatham Marine reporting station, an ingenious tower, which he had to reduce in height in order to get under telephone wires and the strings of signals which formed the street decorations.*

After a gap of one day, the celebration ended on Sunday with sermons written for the occasion.

After all the bills were paid for the bicentennial (which cost $3,023.38 and netted a balance of $143.37 to fund the commemorative book), some writers saw the event as making people think of Chatham in a new way. Chatham natives who had made good in the wider world returned home to be fêted as kings. Townspeople and summer folk alike celebrated in a jubilant mood. Two months later, the Boston Red Sox defeated the New York Giants in the World Series. Despite the lack of opportunity for its young people, Chatham seemed like a pretty wonderful town after all in 1912.

The town's 1912 bicentennial celebration continued well into the evening, with a reception at the Old Town Hall illuminated by electric lights. Little did townspeople know that life would soon change forever. *Photo courtesy of the Chatham, Massachusetts Historical Society.*

In the early days, Chatham's position on the elbow of Cape Cod strongly influenced its development.

Alice Richards Fuller, who moved to Chatham when she married and had seen bodies of drowned men carried off the beach, described the area near the lighthouse to her brother in England in February 1899. "We get the winds right off the Atlantic Ocean and let me tell you they are fearful strong, sometimes tear up trees and everything else in their way, we have some terrible storms," she wrote.[25]

> *But then we have a good many pleasant days, too, and in summer we have such lots of summer company. They come to the seaside to spend their vacations, and think the Atlantic breakers are grand. Well, so they are but in winter they are cruel, too.*

In 1912, geography was beginning to combine with technology to create a new Chatham. In an obvious way, electrification and the arrival of the automobile would do a great deal to change daily life. "To be sure most summer visitors arrived by train and stayed for at least half the summer,"

Joshua Nickerson II recalled.[26] But gradually, in the period of World War I, as Ford's Model Ts rolled off the assembly line and as federal funds became increasingly available to improve roads, "auto traffic took over, at first only chauffeur-driven cars of the wealthy, but soon owners driving family cars."

As early as 1914, the local doctor, F.B. Worthing, was driving a Studebaker car. He wrote a testimonial letter to the *Boston Medical and Surgical Journal* extolling the virtues of an "extra jet" mechanism attached to the car's carburetor. "Formerly in ordinary cold weather it has required several primings and countless, exhaustive spinnings in order to start the motor." But with the "extra jet," which was manufactured by Weld Manufacturing Company, whose factory was next to Chatham's train station, Dr. Worthing could start his car "on the second turn of the crank." During World War I, the company founded by inventor C. Gould Weld turned out parts for artillery shells. The firm went bust in 1918 after an uninsured ship was struck by a German shell and sank in mid-ocean, taking with it the company's entire production.

In subtle ways, the invention of the airplane and radio communications would also change Chatham by bringing an influx of outsiders to man the Naval Air Station and the Marconi Center during World War I. In 1914, August Belmont opened his new Cape Cod Canal, and this, too, changed Chatham, as ships no longer routinely had to pass around the dangerous shoals by Monomoy.

Chatham Electrifies

During the days after the hoopla of the bicentennial died down, no doubt someone observed, as people do today in the waning days of summer, that the nights were drawing in earlier and earlier and dawn was coming later. "Nights were dim before we had electricity," wrote Fred Wight, the only son of Alice Stallknecht, who edited his mother's unpublished memoir *Something of My Past* and added reflections of his own.[27] In looking back, "I see many nighttime glimmers of candles," Wight wrote.[28] "My father thought candles much safer than hand lamps, for if dropped they went out." Throughout the centuries before houses were electrified, fires caused by flames were frequent in the home. (Sparks from passing trains often caused outdoor fires.) In February 1913, the town debated entering into a contract to electrify the town "for a term of five years at a cost to the said Town not to exceed $1000 each year" beginning in 1914 and continuing through 1917. Townspeople tabled the motion but did allow a committee of seven men, including the three selectmen and Heman Harding, to explore the issue of electrification.

In retrospect, electrification seems an inevitable and positive development. At the time, however, it didn't look that way. The year before, in Hyannis, townspeople vigorously debated both sides of the issue and resolved nothing. "Hyannis has been considering the proposition for the past six months, and today is no nearer the lights than when the agitation commenced, not withstanding the project has been before the citizens of the Hyannis Fire District at several public meetings during that time," noted a May 13, 1912 piece in the *Barnstable Patriot.* As the writer wisely concluded, "The dawn of public improvements comes slowly, but when adopted it is but a short time when every one wonders how we got along without them so long."

Unlike Hyannis, Chatham's adoption of electrical power was nearly painless. The committee worked rapidly, and on April 14, 1913, at 7:30 p.m., the town convened to hear Selectman Josh Nickerson's report. (Selectman Nickerson was the uncle of the memoir writer Joshua Nickerson II.) The committee had come to some definite conclusions during its seven meetings.[29]

Nickerson reported that the committee had found that three options were possible. The town could establish its own municipal plant for $20,000, with an annual cost of $4,000 to $5,000. Or it could pay $12,000 for poles, wires and meters, with an annual maintenance fee of $3,000, and then purchase the electricity to flow through those circuits from an outside source. Finally, the town could turn to a franchise, namely the Buzzards Bay Electric Company, a group that was already supplying power to parts of the Cape, including Hyannis, and had a proven track record. A "connection with them would ultimately bring all night and day service," Nickerson noted. With one dissenting vote, the townspeople voted to allow selectmen to grant the franchise to the Buzzards Bay Electric Company for lighting.

"There is no sign yet of electric lights," Heman Harding reported to his cousin H. Fisher Eldredge on New Year's Day 1914.[30]

On March 3, 1915, the *Barnstable Patriot* reported that Erastus Bearse—who, as well as serving as a representative in the Massachusetts legislature, was a jeweler and a prosperous real estate man—leased a tract of land near the *Monitor* office "for a building connected with their electric lighting plant." On the same day, the newspaper reported that "at the hearing in Town hall last Saturday afternoon regarding the erection of poles for the electric light wires, there was practically no objections raised by any of the property owners."

Buzzards Bay Electric was busy, too, as three months later "the trunk pole line of the Buzzards Bay Electric Co. that is being built from Falmouth to Chatham has been constructed to the neighborhood of Shoot Flying Hill in Barnstable."

In 1916, the town allocated $763 to Buzzards Bay for streetlights and an additional $235 to wire the town hall (which was unfortunate, as the building was to burn down three years later). The local committee was also charged with determining which streets would first be electrified, and it chose parts of Main, Cross and Atwood Streets and parts of Old Harbor Road. A book on the historic houses of Chatham claims that Heman Harding's Main Street house was the first in town to be electrified.[31]

Ladies in North Chatham had formed a sewing circle to sell their work to raise funds for public improvements. By carefully investing their funds, the Old Harbor Home Circle raised enough money to electrify areas in North Chatham, the *Monitor* reported in May 1919. "The service on the streets of that village is now maintained at the expense of the Circle."

At first, Joshua Nickerson II recalls, electricity was provided for lighting only and went off at about 11:00 p.m.[32] Power was erratic, and town officials met repeatedly with officials from Buzzards Bay to hammer out problems. Yet by 1916 the Buzzards Bay Electric Company was taking out ads in the *Barnstable Patriot* for household appliances such as electric egg makers (El Eggo), electric percolators and toasters.

In March 1919, the *Monitor* reported that Sea View Street was lighted by electricity for the first time. And another article boasted that the uses of electricity in the home were boundless: electric pads could be used in the bed instead of hot water bottles. Bathrobes, rugs and blankets could also be heated with electricity. Yet caution was needed, too. "Do not cover an electric globe with paper or cloth. It may start a fire."

In the beginning, electricity customers were charged by the number of light bulbs they used. It would be several years before meters were introduced.

1914 Chatham Bars Inn and Hotels

After the train spur finally reached Chatham in 1887, summer people began to trickle in, eventually arriving in such droves that they redefined the town. As a result of the summer folks, "we Cape Codders were exposed to a greater variety of people than most people who lived in small cities," Joshua Nickerson II wrote. "This was very stimulating intellectually and socially, as well as economically."[33]

Although Chatham had always had its summer folk, the town was not one of the great nineteenth-century resort towns—unlike Newport, Bar Harbor

A postcard shows the front of the 1914 Chatham Bars Inn, circa 1928. The Shore Road building, which faces the Atlantic, looks much the same today. *Photo courtesy of the Chatham, Massachusetts Historical Society.*

and the Berkshires, fashionable people had not flocked here. Since Chatham's visitors arrived by train, they had no local transportation, and their activities revolved around the life of the hotel and whatever they could reach on foot. The luxurious Hotel Chatham opened in 1890 with a commanding view of Pleasant Bay. But the hotel was about five miles outside of Main Street—a tremendous distance in the days of traveling by carriage, horse or on foot over sandy roads. As Chatham native Alice Smith said during a 1950s oral interview, "The guests couldn't just sit on the veranda of the hotel and look at the view all day, day after day."[34] The hotel went bust after just two seasons. The Hotel Mattaquason, which opened in town in 1901, fared better.[35] And then came the Chatham Bars Inn.

The Chatham Bars Inn was the brainchild of Boston stockbroker Charles Hardy, a descendant of Chatham's "Squire" Richard Sears, the largest real estate owner in Chatham in the eighteenth century. Hardy formed a syndicate and hired Boston architect Harvey Bailey Alden, a graduate of the Massachusetts Institute of Technology's School of Architecture, to design a three-story hunting lodge that would overlook the Atlantic Ocean. Between

Just east of this spot is where the Hotel Chatham once stood, overlooking Pleasant Bay. The 1890 hotel, built about five miles from Main Street, was ahead of its time and failed in those pre-automobile days. *Photo by the author.*

1913 and 1914, the main inn, nine cottages and a golf course were built. Many townspeople received an invitation:

> *Mr. Charles Ashley Hardy and the management of The Chatham Bars Inn request the pleasure of the company of yourself and family at the informal opening of the Inn on Tuesday, June ninth, nineteen hundred and fourteen at four o'clock in the afternoon.*[36]

As a result, "several hundreds and possibly more than a thousand availed themselves of this first opportunity to look the hotel over." Ice cream and cake were served to the music of John Fogg's orchestra of Brockton. All were "highly delighted."[37]

World events conspired to make the Chatham Bars Inn an early success. War in Europe meant that Americans who were accustomed to doing so could no longer travel abroad. Mrs. Irene J. Boyd, innkeeper at the Hawthorne across the Boulevard from Chatham Bars Inn, predicted a booming business for Chatham and all seashore resorts during the summer of 1915, the first full wartime summer.

But after all, there was no need to set sail for Europe. The Chatham Bars Inn, an early brochure said, was "practically surrounded by water, its broad piazzas and terraces afford the pleasures of a trip at sea."

A large assembly room, hall and dining room took up the bulk of the public space on the inn's first floor, which was "devoted to light and air." A terrace taking advantage of the ocean view extended the entire length of the building, with a dining terrace outside the dining room. On the second floor, "plastered, sound-proof rooms" were priced according to whether they overlooked the nine-hole golf course or had a private piazza overlooking the ocean, with corner rooms costing more. Rooms had hot and cold running water, steam heat and long-distance telephones. Some had "open fireplaces," and private baths with fresh and salt water, which was at the time thought salubrious, were available. Rates could be negotiated by the month or the season. Eighteen private cottages were also available "by special arrangement."

Rates were given for "table board," as well as maids, chauffeurs and valets. A garage offered to rent autos at the rather steep rate of six dollars for the first hour with six passengers or less (food for the week cost $17.50). Private cars could be stored for one dollar a night in a fireproof garage with room for eight cars, washed, polished and furnished with gas and oil. The brochure extolled the benefits of arriving in a car. "Cape Cod is now fully provided from Boston to Provincetown with tarred roads, and presents beautiful scenery to motorists. Nine-tenths of the ninety-mile trip from Boston to Chatham via Plymouth is along the shore."

Another early brochure for the inn begins with an illustrated two-page idyllic essay on Cape Cod, quoting heavily from Henry David Thoreau's 1860s *Cape Cod*, despite the fact that Thoreau never wrote about Chatham in the book. Finally, the unknown brochure writer rhapsodizes of Chatham:

> *Its picturesque streets and quaint houses are always charming pictures, and on the ocean side every coastwise ship has to sail between the dreaded Shovelful and Pollock Rip lightships, which brings them full in view of Chatham town, about a mile off shore.*

The writer launches into tales of shipwrecks on "a shore so terrible," where "the black fish and the smelt are alike stranded by its retreating tide." How wonderful to sit safe on the shore in the summer and watch the dangerous spectacles!

For Chatham's residents, the water was anything but picturesque. In January 1916, the *Monitor* reported, twenty-seven-year-old Harry C. Crowell

A sport fisherman admires the day's haul of five big bass, probably during a fishing trip to Monomoy in the 1930s. When the federal government took Monomoy over as a bird preserve, many who kept camps there protested. *Photo courtesy of Ted Whittaker.*

was winding up a day of fishing with his brother-in-law, Captain Clarington Eldredge, when his foot became entangled in an anchor rope as he pulled in the anchor. Crowell was dragged overboard into the icy waters. Those left on the ship tried to free him from the rope, but when he was pulled from the water, he was dead. Decorating Crowell's casket were flowers in the design of a large anchor.

But the summer folk were not engaged in anything more dangerous than sport fishing, sailing and golfing. Amusements at the inn included tennis playing on three clay courts, bathing in the ocean or a pool, fishing, sailing, motorboating, shore bird shooting and yacht racing on Baybird class boats. Chatham, the brochure later declares in a truth-stretching moment, "offers the most equable climate in New England. There is always a breeze, and the thermometer registers about 72-degrees all summer." Those were, after all, the days before air conditioning.

A scourge of infantile paralysis created a "feeling of unrest and fear among our inhabitants, especially the summer colony," in 1917, but the threat eventually abated.[38]

The inn sold "the best New England cooking," which emphasized seafood and fresh vegetables. In August 1916, during the inn's third

Dining at the Chatham Bars Inn, 1918. *Standing (left to right)*: Walter Marsh, Herbert Doane, Ambrose Nickerson, Mary Woodhouse Eldredge, Abbie Nickerson, Thomas Nickerson and Maro Jones. *Seated*: Miss Marsh, Mrs. Walter Marsh, Mrs. Herbert Doane, Mrs. Ambrose Nickerson, William Eldredge, Mrs. Lewis Doane and Lewis Doane. *Photo courtesy of the Chatham, Massachusetts Historical Society.*

season, the breakfast offerings, served between 7:30 and 9:00 a.m., were heavier than a diner today would expect, with clam bouillon, broiled sirloin steak, honeycomb tripe and breaded veal cutlets sharing a menu with eggs, griddle cakes, popovers, tea, coffee and cocoa. "Clean dairy milk, cream and butter" were provided by "model" Cape Cod farms. In fact, the hotel operated its own twenty-five-acre dairy and produce farm about a mile away.

"I saw a fat man t'other night down at the Chatham Bars Inn putting away a healthy meal, and the man behind the counter told me that he was a self-made man," wrote a Naval Air Station sailor in a 1918 *Monitor* column published under the moniker "K.N. Ocker." "I surely thought so by the amount of food he was putting away. If that is the case someone must have picked up a handful of mud and thrown it in a machine to make all of the men at this place."

The Ladies Find Culture

When the summer folk went back home, Chatham once again returned to its quiet ways. Yet the women had a bit more leisure time than they did during the nineteenth century, and they craved intellectual stimulation.

In 1911, several women met at the home of Alice Walker Guild to form the Ladies' Reading Club. Present were many young mothers who "all shared in common a longing for the wider horizons of art study and reading."[39] Included in that charter group were Josephine Atkins, who would go on to earn a PhD at Boston University and also be ordained; Dr. Minnie Buck, the town's dentist; Florence Smith, the wife of historian William C. Smith; and Eglantine Nickerson, the mother of memoirist Joshua Nickerson II. The group, which restricted itself to twenty members, met every Friday evening during that first year. The women proclaimed:

> *We are not a fashionable woman's club with a dozen schemes for reforming the world in general and man in particular but just a little company of women seeking by united effort to make our reading of greater benefit to ourselves.*

During early meetings, the group tackled topics such as Venice, with particular attention to the damage "being done by the Austrian airship raids," Italian opera and the nineteenth-century writer Thomas Carlyle.

If the Ladies' Reading Club were not enough, in 1914 forty-five women met at Florence O'Neil's house to discuss founding a women's club. The group again included Josephine Atkins and also Margaret Gigger, whose husband was a doctor in town. The objective of the group was "to broaden and strengthen the moral, social, and intellectual life of Club members and to be a power in the community."[40] A year later, the group was officially welcomed into the state federation of Woman's Clubs. To this day, local women belong to both the Ladies' Reading Club and the Chatham Woman's Club.

Marconi Wireless and the Radio Station

While Charles Hardy was busy building Chatham Bars Inn, the Marconi Wireless Telegraph Corporation of America was nosing around a very different site, overlooking Ryder's Cove, in Chatham Port.

Several years before, in 1901, the company had set up a wireless station in South Wellfleet. Problems such as the eroding banks at the site led the company to look around for another location. In 1914, company officials contacted Heman Harding to begin clearing the titles held on the Chatham Port acreage to sell it to Marconi. Complicating Harding's research was the fact that some of the small parcels of land had been held in the same family for over two hundred years.[41]

Harding worked diligently, untangling the old deeds and arranging for rights of way. In the fall of 1914, he sent the company a bill for his work. John Bottomley, the company's vice-president and treasurer, sent Harding $1,000 but balked at the remainder (nearly $600). "I regret extremely that the Directors think that the bill which you have sent us is very heavy indeed and I am anxious to know whether you cannot reduce this bill and accept the amount which I have already sent you in settlement thereof," Bottomley wrote, adding, "You will naturally know that it is distasteful for me to write to you this way."

In November, Harding responded, "I do not feel that my bill is out of the way." The wrangling continued through the holidays and into the new year. "I do not see any reason why I should rebate [the charges]," Harding wrote to Bottomley on February 2, 1915. "I have been ill for seven weeks, a part of it being due to the way in which I was pushed forward on this work for the Marconi Company last Spring."

Maddeningly, the document file trails off without revealing how the dispute was resolved. In any event, in July 1915, the Marconi corporation received a permit to string its wires and construction began. The company erected over fifteen large brick buildings to house the offices and lodging of the radiomen. Also, "half a dozen tall, steel poles of 'masts' have been erected, great tangles of wires have been strung across these far above the ground, and some of the aged sea captains of the Cape are marveling at the wonders of the age, and the gigantic undertaking which means the outlay of so much labor and money," a 1915 article in *Cape Cod Magazine* gushed. The six masts ran in a straight line from Chatham Port to West Chatham. The one in Chatham Port was built on a hill and peaked at 477 feet above sea level; ships forty miles out to sea could see its flashing light. (Most of the masts would be dismantled in 1919, when it was discovered that they were unnecessary for the wireless operations.)

The Marconi Company operated the ship-to-shore radio station for only a couple of years before the U.S. government took over operations for the duration of World War I and brought more strangers to town.

The Great War and the Naval Air Station

The Cape Cod Canal opened in August 1914, the same month that political affairs boiled over in the Balkans, sparking the Great War. In Chatham, Heman Harding organized a Home Guard of sixty-two citizens who would be instructed in rifle practice and investigate strangers. Shortly after the United States entered the war in April 1917, the U.S. Navy announced that a thirty-six-acre tract of land in Nickerson's Neck would be used as a seaplane and blimp base. This remote part of Chatham lay about half a mile beyond where the Hotel Chatham had failed.

The area was deemed appropriate because it was sheltered and had a lengthy sandy beach on Pleasant Bay. In late August, general contractors Coleman Brothers of Boston began construction of living quarters, hangars, gas holders, a boathouse, a dispensary, a pigeon loft and repair shops. Water was piped in from a distance of three and a half miles. The Buzzards Bay Electric Light Company ran poles and wires through Harwich to light up the base. Finally, on Sunday, October 28, the public was invited for the first raising of the American flag at the Naval Air Station. Three thousand residents came on foot for the festivities.

The Naval Air Station was strategically placed to protect Nantucket Sound and the approaches to Boston Harbor from enemy attacks. The nearest known approach of the enemy came on July 21, 1918, when German U-boat *156* attacked the tug *Perth Amboy* off Orleans. Two planes from Chatham responded, dropping bombs that were duds. After a debacle worthy of the Keystone Cops, *U-156* escaped; it was later bombed in the North Atlantic.

During the next few years, the sailors based at the Naval Air Station, like the radiomen at the Marconi Station, formed an integral part of Chatham's social life. In a September 3, 1918 column titled "Hops from the Air Station," "K.N. Ocker" wrote:

> *Now that the summer girls are going there will have to be some tall explaining and rectifying for some of the fellows that have left the town stock during the summer, to get back into the good graces of the old girls to insure a good time for some of the cold nights that are coming. Better start soon, boys, it will take some time for you.*

While out-of-towners were making whoopee with local girls, local boys "have left town to obtain employment in munitions and other factories in order to help win the war," the *Monitor* reported. Edward S. Bearse was the first casualty of the war from Chatham. And Alice Guild's stepdaughter,

"And there'll be lots and lots of the flying men—the what-do-you-call-'ems—aviators, and officers in uniform—and all sorts. What fun! I'm just crazy about uniforms!" says Maud in Joseph C. Lincoln's *Shavings*. Men at the Naval Air Station, 1918. *Photo courtesy of the Chatham, Massachusetts Historical Society*.

Helen, a young woman in her mid-twenties, served as a nurse for six months in France.

The Army and Navy Club bought the former home of Mrs. H.E. Jepson on Cross Street and began holding social events there for the men at the Naval Air and Radio Stations. Both Heman Harding and Joseph Lincoln served on the club's executive committee.

At the end of October, Ensign E. Lingard, who served as gunner on an air mission, died. The plane he was riding in with two other men had landed at sea but could not taxi. The trio was picked up after twenty-seven hours in the water; a few days later, Lingard developed pneumonia. Two hundred sailors from the station marched five miles to the Chatham funeral home and then escorted Lingard's casket to the railroad. Lingard was loaded onto the train to the sound of taps. He was buried in a cemetery in Annisquam.[42]

In May 1919, the navy seaplane NC-4, which had put in for repairs at the Naval Air Station, took off and, with its crew of five, a few days later completed the first west–east transatlantic flight. A year later, the station would be changed to non-operating status, and it finally closed in 1922. Lieutenant Arthur D. Brewer paid homage to Chatham in the *Fly Paper*, calling the town "small, but real."[43]

La Grippe

By the summer of 1918, the Great War was winding down and life seemed to be returning to normal. The boys at the Naval Air Station kept the local girls busy with dances and festivities while the local boys served overseas. On July 2, both Chatham Bars Inn and the Hotel Mattaquason opened for the season. A few days later, a sailor from the Air Station ordered a "baseball fan's breakfast" at Chatham Bars Inn. When the waiter admitted that he didn't know what that was, the sailor said, "Bring me some batter cakes and a pitcher of syrup."[44]

Just after Labor Day, Captain Cooke, the famous Arctic explorer living in Provincetown, came to Chatham and gave his "celebrated lecture" on whaling at the Orpheum Theatre as a benefit for the American Red Cross, the *Monitor* reported. Another benefit for the Red Cross that fall was a play called *The Scallop Shanty: A Chatham Play* by Carol Van Buren Wight.[45] As a classicist, Wight christened his characters with a weird assortment of names such as Miriam, Ichabod, Gabriel, Roxanna, Vashti, Iphigenia and Charley; the goddess Venus also made a cameo appearance.

A woman, Mrs. Josephine F. Merrifield, was appointed principal of the high school "because of an almost impossibility to find a man principal," superintendant Loring G. Williams wrote in the 1919 town annual report. (Charles Guild had departed in 1914 for a more lucrative post, temporarily leaving his wife Alice and children settled in Chatham, to which he would eventually return in retirement.)

Carol Wight's play *A Hole in the Fence* was produced on April 24, 1916. In the back row are (left to right) Gladys Atwood, Carol Wight and Barbara Howes. In the front row are Elizabeth Cowan, Ethel Eldridge and Helen Bearse. *Photo courtesy of the Chatham, Massachusetts Historical Society.*

Under the chairmanship of Joshua Nickerson II's mother, Eglantine, local ladies in the Red Cross had spent a busy three months. By September, they had sent an impressive list of items to the boys overseas. These included 6 pairs of pajamas, 12 convalescent gowns, 72 pinafores, 6 house gowns, 300 knit bags, 31 sweaters, 22 mufflers, 312 pairs of socks, 4 pairs of bed socks, 8 blankets, 5 caps, 12 pairs of wristlets, 7 washcloths, 66 oakum pads, 50 Scultetus bandages, 105 triangle bandages, 6 T-bandages, 23 abdominal bandages, 50 absorbent pads, 2 knitted bandages, 4 head bandages, 400 four-by-four gauze wipes and 125 four-by-four gauze compresses. "Eight testaments and scripture booklets have been sent to be put in the kit bags," the *Monitor* reported on September 3, 1918. The total cost of this was $719.30.

Now that Labor Day had passed, "the absence of automobiles in town on Sunday was very noticeable," the *Monitor* reported that same day. "They have come to Chatham in large numbers all summer Sundays."

In his bicentennial speech of six years earlier, the Honorable James W. Hawes had uttered a few words that might haunt anyone remembering them six years later. In speaking of the smallpox epidemic of 1765–66, Hawes said that "modern science has robbed [smallpox] of its terrors," apparently referring to vaccination programs to eradicate smallpox. But an epidemic more virulent than smallpox lay on the horizon.

They called it Spanish influenza. La Grippe. The plague. And, most sinisterly, "Black Death" because through cyanosis, an inability of the lungs to oxygenate blood, its victims became so bluish black at the time of death that one could no longer determine their race. The illness was believed to have originated in Spain, although by the end of October 1918, Spanish authorities denied that it had originated in Spain. With the hindsight of nearly a century, some medical researchers now believe that what would become a worldwide pandemic may have originated in Kansas, of all places, in the spring of 1918.[46] Other researchers believe that the source of the virulent mutant virus was Canton, China. In any case, slowly but surely, aided by the travel of soldiers and the proximity in which both soldiers and war workers lived at home, influenza insinuated itself into the worldwide population. In the United States, an estimated 675,000 died, with half of those deaths occurring between mid-September and early December 1918. "Never since the Black Death has such a plague swept over the world," the *Hyannis Patriot* noted that month.

Life may have seemed normal for wartime, but it was not. On September 7, a sailor arrived at Camp Devens, thirty-five miles northwest of Boston, complaining of severe body aches—and this was to reverberate throughout

Massachusetts. Meanwhile, Chatham Bars Inn closed for the season on September 9. Augustus M. Bearse, chairman of the Chatham Fuel Committee, took out a newspaper notice asking Chatham residents to conserve fuel. And an unnamed person, presumably a woman, took out an ad saying, "Lost! A ladies' large black hat with green wings. The finder please call telephone 67-2, Chatham." "Our summer guests are fast leaving us, but the increasing number at the camp makes things pretty lively about town," the *Monitor* reported on September 10.

A political season was brewing, too, with Erastus Bearse throwing his hat in the ring in a Republican primary for the Second Barnstable District seat against Selectman William C. Smith, the town historian. In November, Bearse would win the seat.

By late September, hundreds of soldiers and sailors at Camp Devens were sick and dying, as were the nurses and doctors tending them. Worse, the flu was galloping into the general population. The virus was spread through a sneeze or a drop of mucous and came on so suddenly that many people remembered what they were doing when they were taken ill. Symptoms included mucous membranes in the nose and throat, as well as eyelids, becoming enflamed. Then began an intense headache, body aches, fevers up to 103 degrees, exhaustion, coughing, chills and sometimes vomiting. It became difficult to breathe. In the most horrible cases, blood trickled or spurted from the body.[47] The incubation period for the flu was twenty-four to seventy-two hours, and it was "as dangerous as poison gas shells," the *Monitor* advised on October 29.

"The public schools, Orpheum theatre, churches and all public places in town have been closed by order of the Board of Health on account of the grip," the *Monitor* reported on October 1. Already, a Chatham man named Donald Small had died at home. "Death was caused by the grip."

With Boston in the midst of the epidemic, people believed that they were safer away from areas of concentration. "Mr. Collins B. Taylor and family of Cambridge have returned to Chatham for a few weeks on account of the prevalence of the grip in the city," the *Monitor* reported on October 1. A week later, the return of Mr. A.M. Meincke to his Bridge Street home was noted. Meincke would stay in Chatham "until later in the season, not wishing to leave town while the epidemic is raging in the west." Sick with the flu were Elmer Ellis and Joseph W. Nickerson and his family.

Joshua Nickerson II and his classmate Fred Wight began college that fall. The two boys had graduated together from Chatham High School in a class of six. Fred presented an essay, "Kipling's Greatness," and Nickerson gave the valedictorian's speech. Nickerson departed a few days early for his freshman year at Harvard to stay with his sister and her husband in South Weymouth and took in the launching of a submarine from Fore River Shipyards in Quincy. "At midday dinner I did not feel well, left the table and went to lie down," he recalled.[48] "That was the last thing I really knew until several days later, I had influenza, and I was lucky to be alive." Nickerson's father, Oscar, went up to Boston to attend to his son, the *Monitor* reported on October 1.

But Chatham was far from safe. The same issue reported the death of the young man Charles E. Young, known to all from his work delivering the Sunday papers. Unlike the death curve of a classic influenza, half of all those who died were in the prime of life, in their twenties and thirties.

Despite this, when Chatham residents learned that Bulgaria had surrendered, "bells were rung, whistles blew, flags were raised and general enthusiasm prevailed," the *Monitor* reported on October 1.

That was half the trouble—those public gatherings fostered the spread of influenza. "Avoid unnecessary gathering," the Chatham Committee on Public Safety warned the public. "Avoid the cough and the sneeze. Wash the hands frequently and before putting them to the mouth. Keep in the open air and the sun." Those with the flu were instructed to use paper cups and plates, which should be destroyed. Those attending the ill were told to wear cheesecloth masks. Houses were fumigated after a death by lighting formaldehyde candles.[49]

"Our local physicians seem to have the grip well in hand, only a few cases now reported and but one case has proved fatal," the *Monitor* cheerily reported on October 8. "All precautions are being taken and with the fresh winds and salt air with which we are favored let us hope most of the germs will blow off to sea."

By mid-October, the paper reported that Heman Harding's wife, Edith, was recovering from the grip. "The grip sick list is growing less all the time, and we hope to have our town clear of it soon." Churches would again hold services that Sunday, October 20, and schools would open the following day. Despite the horror, the carnival of life continued. On October 15, the *Monitor* reported, "Mr. Charles Train placed on our desk yesterday a freak apple picked from his trees. It is a double apple with one stem, but grown from two blossoms. Call and examine it."

Amazingly, the Naval Air Station attributed only one death to the flu, that of Quartermaster Third Class Joseph D. Yanacek, who died on September 19 of pneumonia.

The war ended officially on November 11, and again Chatham erupted in celebration as church bells rang continuously. "The small children surely acted their part well in providing the street music with horns and old tin pans for drums," the *Monitor* reported on November 12. "At the morning recess the school pupils and the teachers marched through Main Street waving flags at the sound of a drum beaten by one of the pupils. All were overjoyed with the good news."

Mr. James G. Hyde had other matters on his mind. "Notice! I wish to inform the people of Chatham that I do not run a cat farm. Therefore, please do not drop or leave any cats on or near my home."

Medical workers were not immune to influenza, despite the best precautions. Dr. Worthing fell ill and did not recover until after the new year. "Somehow we feel easier when we know the Doctor is well and able to answer when called," the *Monitor* remarked when Dr. Worthing was again seen making his rounds in town a little later.

In December, fifty-eight-year-old real estate man Erastus T. Bearse quit his twenty-five-year position as the third local manager and editor of the *Monitor*. In his resignation letter, he said he thought that the new editor should bring to the attention "of the entire people of this country the many advantages which Chatham possesses both as a place for a summer home or a permanent residence."

The year 1918 ended on an upbeat note, with the Methodists joining the Congregationalists for a Christmas Eve evening service in the Congregational church. "A unique feature of the program was the use of a helmet taken from an Austrian soldier in Italy for receiving a collection to be used for entertaining the boys at the station on Christmas day," the *Monitor* reported.

Christmas Day at the Naval Air Station was, indeed, festive, with Captain and Mrs. Eaton entertaining those left behind for the holidays. A Christmas tree loaded with gifts and goodies reached the ceiling. The tree was festooned with electric roses of various colors that made "a beautiful display when all lights were out in the room."

With the influenza epidemic at last subsiding, teachers returned, and the schools opened on time at the beginning of 1919.

Dear Old Chatham

The Great War had ended. Seven of Chatham's boys had died to keep "the freedom of the world from German tyranny." The flu epidemic was over—only 8 cases of disease came to the attention of the Board of Health in 1919 as opposed to a whopping 175 cases the previous year. It seemed that normal life could resume again.[50]

Early in January, the Ladies' Reading Club met with several of Chatham's "practical, shrewd business thinkers"—all men—to hear their opinions on the war. Oscar Nickerson invoked the Golden Rule, saying, "All nations have sinned and this war was a punishment we all deserved." A woman in the audience was heard whispering, "How can we apply the Golden Rule to a pack of wolves?" the *Monitor* reported.

And then, on January 9, Chatham Town Hall burned to the ground.

The previous evening, a dance had been held in the second-floor hall, which was used for dances, entertainments, graduations and town meetings. At about midnight, after the dance ended, the janitor, Mr. E.Y. Hammond, inspected the building and went home. At about 4:00 a.m. George Bearse and his wife saw flames, but by then it was too late. The *Monitor* speculated that either a stray cigarette carelessly tossed into a wastebasket or an arsonist began the blaze.

A high wind was blowing, "which carried the sparks over in the direction of the Village and endangered the larger part of the Town, but the damp condition of the roofs prevented a general conflagration," William Smith noted in his selectman's record book.

Destroyed along with the 1877 town hall were all of its outbuildings. Also destroyed were the old hearse, the road machine, the oiler and many other tools. The only salvageable items were the contents of various safes, although the safes themselves were ruined. Sadly, "the library of handwritten Reports, the law books, stationery, blanks, typewriters and many other conveniences in the Selectmen's office, outside the safe, were destroyed," Smith wrote. But "the annual report of the Selectmen had been completed and mailed to the Printer before the fire, and no part of the official report of Town officers was destroyed."

Chatham's Old Town Hall burned down in 1919, taking with it many historic documents. The fire was blamed on a cigarette left to smolder after a dance. A new town hall and school building was completed in 1925. *Photo courtesy of the Chatham, Massachusetts Historical Society.*

Unfortunately, the burning of Town Hall took away the only "fine dancing floor in town," the *Monitor* noted on April 19, 1919. Luckily, Charles A. Vose of Brooklyn soon built and managed a dance pavilion on a plat of land near his Chatham home. When Vose opened the pavilion in June, lines of cars surrounded the building. "Surely Chatham has outlived its reputation for being 'quaint,' 'old-fashioned' and even 'dead,'" the *Monitor* crowed in June.

At the end of the month, Heman Harding, Oscar Nickerson, William Smith and seven other men met in the office of Augustus M. Bearse to form the Chatham Board of Trade "to promote the business and society interests of the inhabitants of the Town of Chatham."[51]

In September, the town turned out for "Welcome Home Day." The trees were decorated with flags and bouquets of red, white and blue flowers. Fifty-six of seventy-two soldiers and sailors who had served marched in the parade. William Smith began a speech in preparation of awarding medals, but rain cut him off. The group moved into the Orpheum Theatre, and according to the *Monitor*:

> *Mr. Smith spoke briefly but earnestly putting into words what the townspeople would like to have the day express of their gratitude to the boys for representing Chatham in the Great World War…He said that Chatham's death roll was the longest of any town in the county as she lost one out of every ten.*

As on the commemoration of the 1912 bicentennial, the town made it an all-day affair, following the medal ceremony with a turkey dinner served to 225. And the day ended with a ball at the Vose Pavilion. "It was deplorable that the electric lighting should give out on that evening, but the occasion was a too joyous one to be seriously marred by such an accident," the *Monitor* reported.

The weather turned cold, and on Christmas morning, despite a snowstorm, Mrs. Hawes, who ran the Hawes guest house, received a five-pound tin of sugar from Mrs. Sabie P. Zabriskie of Honolulu who spent several summers at Hawes House. Mrs. Zabriskie said, although she loves Hawaii, her family still longs for "a breath of dear old Chatham," the *Monitor* reported.

And what was Heman Harding doing on New Year's Eve, during the final moments of the decade? Perhaps he was at an early party with his wife, Edith, and returned home in time to tuck in his eleven-year-old daughter, Virginia, "the littlest bear." One wonders if Harding, snapping on an electric light, took a moment to reflect that he was beginning to get his wish: over the past several years, Chatham had come a long way toward opening its doors to visitors. The modern era was about to begin.

THE JAZZ AGE

Oh ain't she sweet,
Well see her walking down that street.
Yes I ask you very confidentially:
Ain't she sweet?

—Milton Ager and Jack Yeller, 1927

Harold Dunbar was crazy about cats. No matter where he lived, he kept a cat, often a big showy tomcat like the yellow-orange Captain Kidd, which liked nothing better than a nighttime brawl out by the trash cans. "Women look at him and shudder," Dunbar once wrote about Captain Kidd, which had lost both ears in a "set-to with a German police dog."[52]

Since the Great War had erupted, ending Dunbar's trips to Italy and France, where he had roamed through small towns and villages with easel, paintbrush and palette in hand, Dunbar had been a summer resident of Chatham. He and his Polish-born wife, Brownie, the former Dorothy May Brownstein, had settled in 1915 where Main Street meets the Boulevard and turns toward the lighthouse. There they opened a tearoom in the house on the corner, where Dunbar sold his canvases right off the walls. Dunbar also taught painting, mainly to a group of ladies and children of varying abilities and talents. During the off-season, the pair returned to Dunbar's studio in Belmont, where Harold continued painting and, when he could, teaching. Over the next four decades, he would dabble in the theatre, try to found an artists' colony and metamorphose himself into a genuine "character." Dunbar, like Lincoln, turned to magazine writing as a way to boost Chatham (and earn money).

Painter Harold Dunbar, who loved cats, on the porch of the Main Street house he rented first from Almena Kent and then from Josephine Atkins. The probable photographer is Dunbar's first wife, Brownie. The couple used the photo as a Christmas card circa 1920. *Photo courtesy of the Chatham, Massachusetts Historical Society.*

The 1920s was a decade of flappers, rumrunners and bootleg gin. It was a time of a bull market and real estate speculation across the Cape. Jazz could be heard over newly invented and mass-marketed radio sets; jazz lured Chatham's younger people into the dance halls that had opened in Chatham after the war. The 1920s simultaneously appealed to the bon vivant in Dunbar's nature and brought out his melancholic streak. At thirty-seven, when the decade began, he was still a relatively young man, slender as ever, and usually seen wearing a hat. In the summer, Chatham perked up as *tomatoes*, the '20s slang term for attractive women, promenaded back and forth in front of his house on their pilgrimages between the beaches and Main Street. After 1923, when Brownie left Harold to pursue an illusive career as an art curator, Harold was free, or would be free, if only he weren't still legally wed.[53]

Harold Crocker Dunbar was born on December 8, 1882, the elder son of Herman and Nellie Bixby Dunbar. The family lived in Brockton, once known as the shoe capital of Massachusetts. Herman worked as a dry goods clerk, but in those days of cheap labor, the family was able to keep a servant, Sela Carlson, from Sweden.

As a boy, Dunbar showed sufficient artistic talent to study at the Massachusetts School of Art and then at the newly formed School of the Museum of Fine Arts in Boston, under Edmund Tarbell, one of the American Impressionists and a founding member of "The Ten." Dunbar polished off his art education in the classic manner, with a stint in Paris at Académie Colarossi. By 1910, he was back in Massachusetts, living in a rented studio on Somerset Street in Belmont and arranging to exhibit his art at the Boston Art Club. In 1913, he married Brownie, whose family lived in Boston. The pair honeymooned in Europe, stopping in Paris and traveling on through the French countryside until the Great War sent them scurrying home again.

Writing once about Brockton, Dunbar noted, "When I was a boy anyone who came from a town smaller than ours was considered slightly inferior."[54] Yet something in Chatham's very small-town atmosphere, which was as dark and quiet as a tomb off-season, cried out to him.

Perhaps it was the people he encountered. Living next door to him where Main Street curved south to the Twin Lights was Josephine Atkins, the orphan girl five years his junior who would be referred to, in future years, as the Gloria Vanderbilt of Chatham because she owned three houses on Main Street and another two in North Chatham, not to mention a cranberry bog, pastures and woodlands.[55]

Miss Atkins, who people much later remembered as the quintessential strict spinster, came from sad beginnings. Emma Josephine Kent Atkins was born on the Fourth of July 1887. Not too long after that, her mother, Lizzie, began treatments in Boston for a brain tumor; she died in November 1889 at the age of thirty. Josephine's father, Captain Joseph Atkins, who spent a great deal of time at sea, asked his cousin, Captain James Kent, and Kent's wife, Almena, to become Josephine's guardians. Then, in April 1900, when Josephine was twelve, her father, now retired from the sea, shot himself through the head. Although her father had remarried several years earlier, Josephine remained with the fifty-seven-year-old Almena Kent.

Josephine and Mrs. Kent lived in a large white house facing east, while the smaller white house they rented to Harold and Brownie faced north. The two houses were connected by an expanse of lawn enclosed by a low white picket fence. Huge silver-leaf poplars separated the property from the road and provided a little shade in the summer. The house where Harold and Brownie ran a tearoom was just across Main Street.

During the couple's first summer in town, Dunbar tramped around the local ponds and beaches with his painting kit and was particularly fond of painting vistas of Mill Pond, with the old mill perched on the hillside. He was also attracted to Stage Harbor's boathouses and oyster shanties. "I believe there is more variety of landscape and interest in Chatham than any other town I have been in," wrote Dunbar, whose words had import since he had, after all, knocked around the world a bit.

Soon, the comings and goings of Harold and Brownie and their friends and relatives were reported in the *Chatham Monitor*. After the summer of 1923, Dunbar stayed on alone in Chatham through the year, and in 1924 he began publishing essays and humorous writings as regular features in several local papers. In 1937, he began to edit a new magazine called the *Cape Cod Beacon* on a somewhat erratic publication schedule.[56] He would go far toward marketing the concept of Chatham as it was evolving into a tourist destination.

And, ultimately, it would be hard to imagine Chatham without Harold Dunbar.

Crash Whiz Bang

"Crash, whiz, bang," wrote Chatham's Fourth of July committee in its ads for the 1923 Fourth gala, but the words might as well have served as the mantra for the Roaring Twenties.

Clearly, as the 1920s began, a reckless tone could be discerned. A page-one headline in the *Chatham Monitor* on January 6, 1920, read, "Girls Buy $300 Fur Coats on Salary of $15 a Week." Those crazy girls! The '20s were already beginning differently, and toward the end of the decade life would be almost unrecognizable to someone who, like a Rip Van Winkle, had been asleep for ten years.

In a year-end round-up article on the same day, referring to the 1919 season, the *Monitor* crowed that "the summer tourist trade had never been better, many people being turned away for lack of accommodations." In the next paragraph, the editorialist noted that during 1919 catches of fish had been "good, prices high." On the other hand, the cranberry crop was not as large as hoped. But a great many people were building houses in town. Summer people, it seemed, not fish, were paramount.

The automobile and its handmaiden—improved, hard-surfaced roads laid by the Massachusetts Highway Commission—made Cape Cod a viable tourist destination. Early in the decade, the Cape Cod Chamber of

Commerce, founded in 1921, began a campaign advertising Cape Cod vacations. "Quaint" was the buzzword—come to quaint Chatham. Old houses and crumbling lighthouses were spruced up with fresh coats of paint. Museums, antique barns, gift shops and summer theatres were established for the new tourist trade.[57]

Prohibition began on January 16, 1920, but whatever Chatham residents thought of the ban on selling, manufacturing and transporting alcoholic beverages under the Eighteenth Amendment, the *Monitor* remained mum. A recurring ad appeared in the paper: Rat-Snap Kills Rats. Meetings were convened on the Lower Cape to deal with the rat problem.

Yet the '20s began less with a roar than with a frigid winter that wouldn't let go. A storm on Christmas morning had taken down the twenty-three-hundred-volt electrical wires that supplied the town with lights. Repairs were made after a night of blackout, and the weather stayed cold. "The ice men anticipate being able to fill their ice houses this winter," the *Monitor* reported on January 6. "Kendrick Bros. began cutting this morning." A week later, enterprising Chatham High seniors, raising money for their spring class trip to Washington, D.C., spotted a crowd skating on Black Pond and sold hot dogs, which they roasted over a bonfire on the banks of the pond.

After a hiatus, William C. Smith was back on the board of selectmen. Real estate values in town had now topped $2.3 million, with 40 percent of

A great snowfall in 1921 brought out a group to shovel on Cranberry Lane in North Chatham. *Photo courtesy of Judith B. Llewellyn.*

the taxes paid by nonresidents. But the town was still counting 71 horses, 126 cows, 24 other "neat cattle" and 3,370 fowl.

The *Monitor* apologized for the paper's late delivery in West Chatham. "The papers have apparently gotten the habit of riding back and forth on the train." New arrangements were made.

At the end of the month,

> *a party of 20 or more young people arranged a sleigh ride to Harwich Thursday evening. The sleighing would not have been considered very much by our neighbors farther north but the young folks were not critical and enjoyed themselves very well.*

The snow delayed trains coming into Chatham. Church attendance plummeted. The streets were coated with ice-covered snow that made walking treacherous. Residents who fell and broke their limbs were dutifully written up in the *Monitor*'s Chatham column. Influenza—the garden variety kind, not the deadly Spanish flu—broke out at the Naval Air Station, causing a quarantine, with twenty-three men lying ill.

A new bank was being built, and the Chatham Electrical Shop installed its lighting system. When Chatham Trust opened on January 15, it did a brisk $120,000 worth of business, with young Walter C. Harty depositing four hundred pennies and receiving Bank Book No. 1.

Those pennies were safe in the bank. "The vault, containing the huge safe weighing six and a half tons, gave the impression of extreme solidity, and one fails to see how a burglar could make much headway trying to open it," the *Monitor* reported on January 20.

Residents hunkered down inside and enjoyed a few parties. Miss Helen Hopkins held a New Year's Eve party for young people in her Main Street home. The group enjoyed musical selections and then played whist. Joshua Nickerson II, home from Harvard for the holidays, shared a first prize. William Smith's daughter, Marjorie, was also at the party, the *Monitor* reported on January 6.

A couple of weeks later, Mr. and Mrs. William L. Drew threw a party for the grown-ups and included Chiefs Moseley and Beattie from the Naval Air Station. Mrs. Drew served raw oysters, Saltines, cake, hot cocoa, apples and chocolate. The *Monitor* reported on January 20:

> *Mrs. Rushton was at the piano and also sang contralto. Mrs. George Steward of Dover, N.H., a daughter of Mr. and Mrs. Drew, and Mrs. Thayer sang soprano, their voices blending so charmingly they delighted the hearers.*

The age of routine musical performances in the home was nearing an end. Within a couple of years, jazz would sweep through the nation courtesy of radio. KDKA in Pittsburgh, the first commercial radio station, began by broadcasting the Cox-Harding election returns on November 2, 1920. Cape Cod would finally get its own radio station, WSGC, broadcasting from the Seapuit Golf Club in Osterville, in July 1926. "At frequent times, summer reception conditions have been so bad at the Cape when tuning in on Boston and New York, that there has long been a call for what may be termed the Cape's own station," the *Monitor* reported in a page-one story in July 1926. Six nights a week (excluding Mondays), the station featured Jim Moynahan's Cape Cod Orchestra, as well as yachting and sports news.

F. Scott Fitzgerald was about to publish a book of short stories called *Tales of the Jazz Age* and lend a name to the entire decade. A 1923 short story, "The Curtises' Grandmother," printed on page one of the *Monitor*, noted that "the youngsters were, to be frank, 'jazz crazy'...Their pocket money went for new records." In Hyannis, records could be bought at Union Furniture Company for seventy-five cents apiece or on sale at three for one dollar. Also available in Hyannis at Louis Dranetz & Company was a new garment called "Ladies Jazz Garters." The first feature-length talking film, opening in 1927, was *The Jazz Singer*, starring Al Jolson. Jazz records could be played on a Pathe phonograph, available at J.F. Quilty's in Chatham.

At the town meeting, held in the Orpheum Theatre by necessity since the town hall still lay in ashes, Heman Harding, who chaired the committee looking into replacing the town hall, unveiled plans. The new building would serve as a community gathering place, with a basement dining hall for 250 with its own kitchen. The main floor would provide an assembly hall for 350, with a stage, ticket office and separate dressing rooms with toilets for ladies and gentlemen, as well as rooms for the selectmen to meet and town offices. A gallery would hold 100 people. If built in colonial brick, it would cost $75,000; if in wood, $50,000. Yet Harding did not recommend building "at this time with all building materials at abnormal prices," the *Monitor* remarked on February 10.

A year later, in fact, townspeople found that such a large complex was not needed—"public gatherings can occur elsewhere"—and recommended a more modest town administration building with modern conveniences for town officers, complete with a police lockup.

Ultimately, the town voted to build a new school on Main Street, with quarters for the town offices in the back. In July 1924, when the cornerstone for the building was laid, town officials watched as a tin box containing a copy of the 1923 town annual report; the *Chatham Monitor* of

May 20, 1924; the 200th anniversary book; and Smith's *History of Chatham, Massachusetts* was buried. A year and a half later, the building committee formally handed over to the selectmen the keys to the new building. "The building is one which gives to every citizen a feeling a pride," the *Monitor* reported on February 10.

Town leaders continued to be preoccupied with funding the lighting of town and the improvement of the roads. Augustus M. Bearse, the town clerk and treasurer, "deplored the impression that visitors must receive when they enter town over a road in as bad condition as Main Street is at present."

And so the harsh winter dragged on with reports of limbs broken as citizens slid on the icy streets. A Mrs. Boyd wrote from St. Petersburg, Florida, describing a kind of Shangri-La of plentiful strawberries, oranges and grapes that sold for ten cents a dozen. "After our struggles with snow, water and ice, we are mostly ready to echo her wish that Chatham people could fly down there and enjoy the sunshine city," the *Monitor* noted.

Something else became apparent, too: Chatham girls were marrying men from as far away as Hampton Roads, Virginia, and Lake Forest, Illinois. Some of those evenings, over Saltines and song with men from the Naval Air Station and the Marconi Radio Station (since the war run by the Radio Corporation of America [RCA]), had led to serious commitments.

Women seemed to want more from life than keeping house might offer. In 1920, with the passage of the Nineteenth Amendment, women were given the right to vote. Something in the very air seemed to be infecting women with ideas. During August 1921, a man named Floyd J. Worth placed a strange notice in the *Monitor*:

> *The notice in last weeks' Monitor of my wife, Mabel S. Worth, that she left the house at my mother's request and my knowledge, and that I promised to support her, is not according to the facts. The reason was that she was influenced by her so-called friends.*

New York Meets Chatham

Far away that winter, in New York City, *Shavings, a Comedy in Three Acts*, based on the 1918 novel *Shavings* by Joseph C. Lincoln, was playing in the Knickerbocker Theatre on Broadway. The play, set during World War I in the fictional town of Orham, centered on an oracular figure named J. Edgard W. Winslow, nicknamed Shavings, who made a living creating toy

Arthur Edwards outside his "Shavings" ball-bearing windmill shop on Old Harbor Road, with tourist Mrs. Megrue, in May 1925. Edwards and his shop were made famous by Joseph C. Lincoln's 1918 novel *Shavings* and the Broadway play of the same name. *Photo courtesy of the Chatham, Massachusetts Historical Society.*

whirligigs. "He was a thin man and his trousers hung about his ankles like a loose sail on a yard," Lincoln described Shavings.[58] "His voice was a drawl, very deliberate, very quiet, rather soft and pleasant."

And thanks to articles in newspapers like the *New York Times*, it was no secret to the canny public that the "real" Shavings—although he initially quibbled over details—was Arthur E. Edwards, who lived on Old Harbor Road. In fact, the stage set of Shavings was "as nearly as possible…an exact copy of your little shop," stage manager John McKee wrote to Edwards.[59] Joseph Lincoln conceded that he had spent time with Arthur Edwards and, in fact, took notes while Edwards spoke.[60]

In 1920, Edwards was a sixty-three-year-old father of four who had spent his entire life in Chatham. A carpenter by trade, he apparently met Lincoln when working on Lincoln's house, Crosstrees, in 1915. Before turning his hand to creating whirligigs, he was an ingenious inventor who had applied for patents on, interestingly, items revolving around transportation, such as an inner tube repair kit and a motorcycle stand. Soon, Edwards was to make tires spin in another direction—toward Cape Cod, where, in the days before celebrity culture, tourists sought out Edwards to take home a souvenir whirligig, a photo of themselves posing with Edwards and an autograph. Theatregoers saw Edwards's mills right in the Forty-second

Street theatre, and they wanted one. In May, the producer, Henry W. Savage, wrote to Edwards asking him to send along another "one dozen mills same as before."[61]

Edwards operated out of a modest one-story building, where eventually dozens of his whirligigs spun in the breeze. His 1920 card read, "Chatham's Old Cape Souvenirs. Ball-Bearing Mills" and showed a sketch of a windmill. The story went that it was Joseph Lincoln's wife, Florence, on a visit to Edwards's shop, who said that a smart man would change the name of the shop to "Shavings" and pick up the New York tourist trade. Edwards was nothing but smart, and he changed the sign to "Shavings."[62]

After that, what was Edwards's shop but a stage, with Edwards in a starring solo role whenever a car drove up filled with out-of-towners? Joseph Lincoln may have written the original script, but Edwards ad-libbed brilliantly.

The copy in a *New York Times* ad for a Fifth Avenue florist described a meeting with Edwards. "At first he was mighty closed mouthed"—exactly what we expect of the Cape Codder rather than the slick-talking city man—"but when he finally did loosen up, what a wealth of life's philosophy and keen humor he did have."[63] Over the next two decades, in fact, Edwards would mold himself into a genuine Olde Cape Cod product: the wise old salt. Uncounted tourists would detour into Chatham to pick up a whirligig and some of Edwards's life philosophy to share with the envious folks back home.

Church Bash: August 1920

Chatham was a town that knew how to do things right. In 1912, it had celebrated its bicentennial with a three-day bash. Now the town's oldest church, an institution as intertwined with the town's history as William Nickerson himself, was celebrating its own 200th birthday on August 6, 7 and 8.

Months before the celebration, a committee and subcommittees convened to decide such vital issues as who would speak, what events would be held and the menu of the dollar-a-plate church supper on Friday evening. William C. Smith, a veteran of the town's bicentennial celebration, chaired the church's anniversary committee and prepared another history, which he read after supper. (The text of his church history, of which 250 copies were printed, runs to twenty-seven pages.)[64]

Back in the days when people's social lives revolved around the church, the church recognized the importance of putting on a good meal. In July, the food committee finalized the menu for the Friday night supper. Late in the month, the committee appointed Hittie Eldredge "to find where to obtain and cost of 100 pounds of fowl." Also on the shopping list were forty dozen rolls, ten packages of mint Jell-O, one gallon of stuffed olives, four pounds of butter, ten loaves of bread, six gallons of ice cream, boiled ham and thirty loaves of cake. Ultimately, the "100 pounds of fowl" was converted to chicken salad and served alongside scalloped clams, sliced ham and sliced tomatoes with salad dressing.

The weekend also featured an exhibition of sixteen "articles of historical interest," at one point referred to, in the notes, as "relics." Mercifully not included were items such as fingers of previous ministers, but the "articles" did include parts of communion services, as well as more eccentric items such as a "piece of fringe used on window drapery sixty or more years ago."[65]

The Dark Side of Town

In the early 1920s, while Chatham residents were just beginning to ponder how to lure in the tourists, darker forces were also at work. It was Prohibition, a time, in the minds of some, to make a buck off the unslaked desire for alcohol. Chatham, with more than sixty miles of coastline, had long served as a haven for those who wanted to earn a buck some other way than through a paycheck. Prohibition provided new challenges and opportunities for those who knew Cape Cod's coast well.

The early days of Prohibition were, in a sense, the most innocent, with one writer claiming that fishermen in Chatham, Provincetown and New Bedford soon learned that bringing in a load of rum paid better than a load of cod. Sometimes the fishermen hauled in a load of booze under a load of fish.[66] Later, as Prohibition dragged on, armed mobs from Boston elbowed into rumrunning, and it became a more dangerous proposition.

In 1922, thirty-two-year-old Everett R. Eldredge of West Chatham was appointed the town's first chief of police—no doubt in part to enforce the Eighteenth Amendment. "The town voted that an out of town man be appointed, but a petition influenced [selectmen] to appoint Mr. Eldredge," the *Monitor* reported on June 6, 1922. The local man would have a major edge over a man from out of town: he would know the shore of Chatham intimately.

Eldredge was a sort of compromise candidate. The son of a Chatham sea captain, he had been educated in Winthrop and had worked at various jobs in the Boston area. For two years, he was proprietor of a poolroom in Dorchester. While there, he fought professionally in the Boston ring under

Frederick Wight's painting *The Bootleggers*. Cape Cod was an active spot for rumrunners and bootleggers during Prohibition. Some believe that the painting depicts the town of Truro rather than Chatham. *Photo by the author from a painting at the Chatham, Massachusetts Historical Society.*

the name Gunboat Eldredge. He married Emily Stearns of Dorchester, and their son, Everett Raymond Jr., known as Gunny, was born in 1912. Eventually, the family moved back to Eldredge's roots in West Chatham.[67]

During Prohibition, liquor was legally stored along Rum Row in vessels moored off Provincetown beyond the twelve-mile limit patrolled by the Coast Guard. The challenge lay in conveying the booze to shore and distributing it on land. When the Coast Guard moved in too close to a rumrunner, he would toss his load overboard. "Only last month cases of alcohol were seen floating in these waters," Dunbar wrote about Chatham's beach in the *Hyannis Patriot* in July 1924. Bottles were "constantly" found on the beach, and as many as four hundred cases appeared in shallow water.[68]

Oscar Nickerson was for many years the town's moderator, presiding at the annual town meeting in February. One year early in Prohibition, his son Joshua recalled, the townspeople were discussing a certain old road that led to the shore. Many voters were confused as to which road it was. Oscar

Nickerson said, "'It is that road, you know, which leads down to the deep hole along the shore, where the rum-runners like to land.' And of course everyone then knew exactly where it was!"[69]

Members of the Monomoy Brant Club invented their own drink during Prohibition, a "Monomoy." The recipe that Joshua Nickerson II gives consists of a lump of sugar, Angostura bitters, Medford rum, a slice of fresh lemon and two or three cloves, all topped with boiling water.[70]

A Nickerson was supposedly caught hauling in a load of booze on Andrew Harding's Lane not far from the Twin Lights. "You could hear the boats sometimes up at our house," a woman who grew up near the lighthouse recalled many years later.[71] "You could hear the motors at night, and lights flashing—off and on." Rumrunners were said to store their booze in unoccupied cottages down at Harding's Beach.

Eldredge, in his 1923 town annual report, lists eight liquor raids in Chatham in 1923, the first year he was chief. In 1925, three arrests for drunkenness—one for driving under the influence and two for illegally transporting liquor—were noted. That same year, the Women's Christian Temperance Union, which met regularly to keep the specter of the dangers of alcohol before its members, sponsored an essay contest with the topic: "As a citizen, what attitude should I take regarding the drinking of alcoholic liquors?"

Liquor also came to town by train. "All the people that wanted liquor had it come down from the city, the box usually marked beans or other grocery items."[72]

In September 1922, a car driven by Chatham resident Charles Vose was badly damaged on Main Street "by a car operated by men from Boston. The Boston men were in no state to be at the wheel of an auto and the crowded Main Street was of no assistance in avoiding accidents," the *Monitor* reported.

A popular movie at the end of 1922, *Over the Border,* told the tale of the daughter of a bootlegger smuggling "wholesale quantities" of liquor from Canada. The young woman's life was complicated when she became the sweetheart of a Royal Mounted Policeman.

While *Over the Border* was playing in local movie houses, the schooner *Salvatrice* and the motor fisherman *Star* were seized in the bay off the Cape Cod Canal. The *Salvatrice*, reported the *Barnstable Patriot* on December 18, 1922, was loaded with two thousand cases of alcohol from Antwerp and had been flying distress signals after getting caught in a storm.

Summer residents Noble Cathcart, editor of the *Saturday Review of Literature*, and friend Bill Barclay tailgate in the back of a 1934 Ford station wagon. Note the beer bottle stuck in the exhaust pipe in the post-Prohibition days. *Photo courtesy of Ted Whittaker.*

A Disposable Culture

If Chatham residents had once quietly tended their houses and cast their eyes to the sea, those days were over. Already, in 1921, in his book *Massachusetts Beautiful*, the former Congregational minister turned photographer/chronicler Wallace Nutting warned against unscrupulous Cape Cod antique peddlers who would fob off a chair with "a pair of front legs that have known each other long but are unacquainted with the legs behind."[73] He remarks that the Great War brought a naval station to Chatham and links this with the deplorable fact that Society-with-a-capital-*S* has arrived on Cape Cod.[74] Yet he, like many other writers, waxes rhapsodic about the "agreeable sleepiness" of some villages—as though Cape Cod is an enchanted place that time forgot. "There is a fine aroma about a quiet old village by the sea not comparable to or equaled by other haunts."[75]

Yet every day, it seemed, as the decade wore on, life changed. Women's hemlines climbed and hovered at mid-kneecap and the corset was no more. The phonograph was getting to be ubiquitous, as were electrical appliances such as the Frigidaire, which had a freezer compartment and by the end of the decade could be bought on an installment plan. The Acme Laundry's ads were geared to Chatham's modern woman, who no longer wanted to spend one day a week hunched over a bucket scrubbing sopping laundry. Voters at town meeting were asked to agree to build a new high school. King Tut's tomb was being excavated near Luxor, and that began a rage for all things Egyptian. On June 12, 1923, the Little Shop in Chatham advertised that the new Egyptian crêpes are here, as well as the "King Tut voiles." As the pace of life increased and became more modern, so grew an awareness that something was being lost: Chatham's past. In 1923, per order of the lighthouse board, Monomoy Point Light was deactivated and eventually bought by George S. Bearse, who had run a garage in Chatham since 1910. Worse, much worse, Chatham's northern Twin Light was moved up the coast to Nauset.

The current white conical Twin Light structures were built in 1877 to replace the brick Twin Lights, which erosion had brought perilously close to the shore. (The original set of Twin Lights was erected in 1808 and made of wood.) A house for the keeper and his assistant was set between the lights.

For 115 years, twin lights had stood in Chatham, lending their name to an entire neighborhood. Sara Ware Bassett, a summer resident of Chatham, wrote a 1934 novel called *Twin Lights* about spinster sisters who divided their house down the middle and burned "twin lights" in the evening.

A postcard of the Twin Lights also shows the Mack Monument. The neighborhood around the lighthouses was referred to as Twin Lights until one light was removed in 1923. Summer resident Sarah Ware Bassett wrote a novel of that title. *Photo courtesy of the Chatham, Massachusetts Historical Society.*

And how was the light actually moved? Shirley Sabin of the Nauset Light Preservation Society dubs the move "the biggest mystery in the world."[76] Unlike news organizations of our day, which would cover the move of the lighthouse from every possible angle, newspapers of the time are mute about the move. Although 1923 lies within the memory of many living people, the recollections of those who saw the lighthouse move conflict. Some believe that it was conveyed by water; others claim that it was moved by land or by water and then land. One witness says that it was moved intact. Based on archaeological evidence, the preservation society believes that the five-ring lighthouse was moved in sections by land. Sabin believes that the ultimate answer to the mystery lies buried somewhere in the National Archives in Washington, D.C., in a dusty, uncatalogued box.

When Chatham Light lost its twin, the beam of the remaining light was changed to a flashing light and increased to twenty-five-thousand candlepower from nine thousand. It was said that the light could be seen from a distance of eighteen miles at sea on a dark night in a clear atmosphere.[77] The light, reached by a circular iron staircase, was lighted every night at sundown. Through the long winter nights the light burned six quarts of kerosene.

The Chatham High School classes of 1906–10 held a reunion in August. "While we all believe in progression," an alumna was quoted as saying in the

Monitor on August 28, "we shall rather hate to see the old school house go, as with our Town Hall already gone and only one twin light left, where can we old time graduates find a place to reminisce? Old friends, like old wine, are best."

And inevitably, the town's old folks were dying off too—the ones who shaped the nineteenth century and most vividly remembered it. Around Labor Day, postmaster William L. Nickerson, credited with bringing the telephone to Chatham, died. (His father, Ziba, once the oldest resident, had died on the first morning of the 1912 bicentennial celebration.) In the 1880s, William Nickerson had established a marine observation station at Chatham that made Chatham's "shoals passable and save[d] ships sailing Cape Cod several hours time," the *Monitor* reported on September 4. Carol Wight wrote a memorial poem about Nickerson: "The twilight of your memory grows not grey."[78] William's wife, Euphemia, erected a monument to William's memory near the lighthouse.

As the past was subsumed and forgotten in a tide of progress, life could be very disorienting. In November 1923, during a meeting of the Ladies' Reading Club, the idea of forming a historical society to preserve Chatham's heritage was raised.

The Chatham Marine Observatory, established by William Nickerson on the corner of Mill Pond Road and Main Street, offered a view of the sea from its tower. An "ingenious" replica of the building was constructed for the 1912 bicentennial parade. *Photo courtesy of the Joseph A. Nickerson Jr. Collection.*

The guiding force behind the historical society was Alice Walker Guild, who first came to Chatham as a teacher for the 1902–03 school year. After a few years away, she returned to Chatham in 1910 and stayed to raise five children. Guild started the Ladies Reading Club in 1911 and remained its president until 1965.

In early December 1923, a group met and Heman Harding was chosen chairman pro tem. The group agreed to draft bylaws for the fledgling institution, which already had thirty members who had paid a fee of one dollar each. The group would hold two meetings a year, in February and August. Alice Guild, local dentist Minnie Buck and Joshua Nickerson II were elected to prepare a program for the February meeting. "This is a good start and the enthusiasm is genuine so that the society feels that it may be able to do its bit for old Chatham," the *Monitor* noted in its Chatham column, which, incidentally, Alice Guild was now writing at the salary of one dollar a week.

During the February meeting, the first papers were presented on the town's old saltworks and windmills. William C. Smith, who was elected president that evening, emphasized hunting for old deeds, which the society would preserve. He also mentioned the neglected slate gravestones dating to the smallpox epidemic of 1765–66 and presumably suggested that members consider ways to preserve them.

A little over a year later, townspeople voted to allow the society to use the lower room in the Atwood School Building. But the following fall, the society called a special meeting in the parlor of the Methodist Episcopal church on Main Street to discuss the purchase of the old Atwood House on Stage Harbor Road. The house was said to date from 1752, making it Chatham's oldest standing residence. "The owner has made the society an offer which seems reasonable and if it is to be preserved as a memorial of earlier days it would seem that now is the time to secure it," the *Monitor* noted.

The house took its name from its original owner, Joseph Atwood, who built the house on thirty acres of farmland. The rare gambrel-roofed house was passed down in the family for several generations. In 1832, John Atwood lured Marjorie Smith into marriage by promising her a new house. "The trusting maiden waited until after the knot was tied and then John said the house was only courtin' talk." Marjorie did, however, get an ell and perhaps a new kitchen.[79]

In 1925, the house was owned by three Atwoods, none of whom lived on Cape Cod or even in Massachusetts. Heman Harding offered the trio $2,000 for the house—about a third of its value—and after they accepted it, Harding took care of the legal details and also incorporated the society.

In the summer, the society solicited contributions and held a fundraiser with "Jitney Players" on the lawn of Joseph Crocker's house. Tickets were $1.65 and $1.10. Little by little, they raised $2,000 to pay for the Atwood House.

The group was soon faced with a second problem—a bill for $1,000 to pay for necessary repairs as the house was in "such forlorn condition."[80] Rather than working hard "getting suppers to earn money to pay someone else" to work on the house, several society members elected to do the repair work themselves. Rebecca Nickerson, Minnie Buck and Alice Guild scoured, painted and patched cracks in the plaster of the side walls. Other ladies filled in nail holes in the woodwork with putty and then painted it with two coats—one of flat white, the other of "Barrelled Sunlight." They wallpapered the first floor. Minnie Buck, the dentist, was handed a can of putty and asked to fix the windows, "a filling job it was asserted should come easily to her. She protested the putty knife as clumsy, wished she had a more familiar small tool, but anyway the glass in the windows set tight when she was through."[81]

The women continued painting and wallpapering, in one room peeling off seven layers of wallpaper. Augustus Ellis cleaned up the grounds, where rubbish such as old boots, clothes, papers, tin cans, ashes and "nondescript articles" had accumulated through the years.[82]

In November 1926, the house opened to the public for the first time, "showing the house as a home." Mrs. William Smith and Mrs. Herman Taylor, wearing "heirloom garments," presided over a candlelit tea table "furnished with heirloom dishes," the *Monitor* reported on November 11, 1926. Visitors admired the house's architectural features. The society's next goal was to collect furniture. Donations of furniture began, with some gifts coming from people unknown to the society, a pleasant surprise. By 1933, the house had been well restored.

As the decade wore on, the society sponsored talks on such topics as daguerreotypes, silhouettes and miniatures. Grace Hardy gave a talk on Chatham's lighthouses. It sponsored bridge parties, at which members sold candy and flowers to raise funds.

And with an eye toward beginning its archives, in November 1925 the society took out a running ad in the *Monitor*:

> *Please do not destroy old wills, deeds, or any other old papers. The Chatham Historical Society desires to make a collection. It will be to your interest to talk with them before disposing of any. They wish copies of reports of town officers from early days to the present.*

Sidewalk Consultations

Despite the increasing numbers of strangers clogging Main Street in the summer, Chatham retained its folksy side. Dr. F.B. Worthing once recalled that he was standing on the sidewalk in front of his Main Street office one fine summer day when a big limousine pulled up. A "nice old lady" opened the back door of the car and asked Dr. Worthing if he knew anything about the doctor in the office.[83]

Dr. Worthing told her that he had known him since he arrived thirty years back.

The lady then asked about the doctor's reputation, confiding that she was considering bringing him in to look at her husband.

"He'd probably be fine, Madam, if you could catch him when he was sober," Dr. Worthing replied. The lady asked if he thought the doctor would be sober now.

In *The Circle Supper*, Alice Stallknecht depicted Dr. Frank Bertell Worthing waiting for his supper of baked beans and brown bread. *Photo by the author from a painting at the Chatham, Massachusetts Historical Society.*

"I told her I was sure he was, because I was the doctor, and at her service." The lady laughed and took Dr. Worthing to the inn to see her husband. "I found out what ailed him, and fixed him up so that he was able to enjoy his vacation."

Frank Bertell Worthing, originally from Kennebec, Maine, came to be a "landmark" in Chatham. "He never wears an overcoat, has eased the ills of everyone of consequence in these parts since time immemorial, and even in Washington, D.C., they have heard of him," Harold Dunbar, wrote in the *Cape Cod Beacon* in April 1937. When Worthing turned seventy in 1940, Dunbar painted a large birthday card called *The Three Landmarks*—they were Chatham Light, the Old Mill and Dr. Worthing.

Dr. Worthing described himself as "an old fashioned country doctor, a bird that is almost as extinct as tallow candles" in the same issue of the *Beacon*. Dr. Worthing often accompanied his patients who needed treatment off-Cape. In January 1921, he traveled with an Atwood to a Boston hospital for an operation. A couple of months later, he accompanied a Nickerson to Wellesley for treatment in a private sanitarium.

During a 1926 measles epidemic, Dr. Worthing, the *Monitor* reported, was recovering from "a hard cold." He held throat clinics in his office to spot those children who needed tonsils and adenoids removed.

Dr. Worthing's office, which was by the post office in the most hectic part of town, was convenient for his emergency work. When Clyde Eldredge stepped backward directly into the path of a car on Main Street, Dr. Worthing was on hand to stitch up the child's head wounds. Through his work examining schoolchildren, the residents of Chatham got to know Dr. Worthing while young. He found the overall condition of the children "excellent" but in need of better posture to be gained through work in a gymnasium. "Sound heads grow better on sound shoulders," he cheerily wrote in his annual report.

In September 1926, another native of Maine, Dr. Carroll H. Keene, always known as Doc Keene, arrived in town and began delivering the first of what he estimated to be between one and two thousand babies over the course of his career. Two years later, Doc Keene married Miss Harriet Camp, and the pair began to raise their two children in Chatham.

Flickering Lights

When Harold Dunbar came down to Chatham in June 1923, Brownie stayed behind in Boston, and in some ways it must have been a relief. He was tired of Brownie spying on him from behind the Coast Guard house as he tried to paint *en plein air* on the beach below the Twin Lights, and he tired of her intense hatred and distrust of his mother. Alone now, Dunbar stayed in the house owned by Mrs. Kent where he and Brownie had lived.

On Main Street, observers during that summer noted license plates from almost every state in the union, with "New Jersey [as] common as Massachusetts" plates. "It is sometimes quite surprising to realize how far Chatham's fame has gone," the *Monitor* remarked on August 7, 1923.

The modern era came haltingly, like a child learning to ride a bicycle, falling and then picking herself up. "It was impossible to sit through any social gathering, the movies or any kind of public meeting without trembling lest the lights should go out," wrote an early historian of electrical service on Cape Cod. Candles were standard equipment in hotels and homes.[84]

"It is hoped that we may soon be able to give our citizens and those visiting us in the Summer better facilities for enjoying the fine bathing to be found along our shores," town officials wrote in the 1922 town annual report.

The summer folk were developing exclusive places for themselves, too. Charles Hardy, whose hotel Chatham Bars Inn had opened in 1914 and remained a success, looked into developing the land on Nickerson's Neck, near the Naval Air Station, as an eighteen-hole golf club. (The Naval Air Station, which was built in 1917, had been decommissioned in May 1920, and during the next few years only a watchman remained at the deteriorating site.) English golf architect W. Herbert Fowler began laying out the course on the breathtaking site overlooking Pleasant Bay in 1920. In July 1922, the country club opened for play. The club originally envisioned 150 members, but financial straits eventually compelled Hardy to buy back the club. Later, summer resident Roy E. Tomlinson, the president of the National Biscuit Company, bought the club for $75,000. "He then politely suggested that his friends should either put up or shut up," Joshua Nickerson II recalled.[85] Within a year, Tomlinson was able to sell it back to members with no profit to himself.[86]

By the end of the decade, as members wanted to raise additional funds for a clubhouse, Joseph Lincoln himself was appointed membership chairman and led a publicity campaign to increase membership and funds. That accomplished, an eighteenth-century house once owned by Ensign Nickerson was moved and formed the basis of the club facilities. Among the forty-eight club members listed in April 1929 were Heman Harding, Joshua Nickerson II and Harold Brett, who illustrated many of Lincoln's novels.

The 1923 Fourth of July parade brought an estimated "3000 strangers" to town. Flags were flying everywhere. One float represented that new invention

The Eastward, Ho! Country Club, established in 1922, became a favorite golfing spot for summer people and town luminaries such as Joseph C. Lincoln. Displayed on the clubhouse walls today are several original oil paintings by Lincoln's illustrator, Harold Brett. *Photo by the author.*

soon to be in every home—the radio. After the parade came games like croquet, followed by a dance for 350 at the Chatham Tea Room. Although the ever-erratic electric lights again failed, it "didn't quench the spirit of the holiday crowd," the *Monitor* reported. Regardless, Cape and Vineyard Electric Company announced that it was planning to invest $100,000 to make electricity more reliable. Although much of the town was now electrified, service remained erratic. "If an exceptionally fat seagull should land on the wires at Buzzards Bay, the Cape might be in darkness for an entire night."[87]

A writer—probably of an older generation—preached in the *Monitor* on August 28, 1923:

> *An occasional and temporary return to oil lamps, while inconvenient, serves to remind some of this generation of what their parents considered almost a luxury, while their grandparents were dependent upon the tallow dip for their household illumination.*

As interest in the town's history increased, the Fourth of July float, 1926, featured Bertha Arey, secretary of the new Chatham Historical Society, and painter Harold Dunbar, both wearing white caps, standing next to an antique spinning wheel. *Photo courtesy of the Chatham, Massachusetts Historical Society.*

The hotels were packed to the gills, especially when, in late July, the cities were broiling. Even in Chatham the mercury hit the one-hundred-degree mark briefly at noon, but "by Sunday wraps were again needed."

At about that time, Heman Harding, trying to sell his in-laws' hotel the Monomoyick after his father-in-law's death, wrote to a prospective buyer: "We have arrived as a summer place. There are many hotels and boarding houses and I know of none which are not succeeding. We badly need more accommodations."[88]

President Warren G. Harding died on August 2, supposedly after an illness resulting from eating tainted crabmeat in Alaska, and a local memorial service was held in the Orpheum. Heman Harding described President Harding as "a simple, kindly, Christian gentleman, another Moses called to lead a chosen people." Not for long would most people think of the late Republican president from Ohio in a favorable light as the details leaked out of the Teapot Dome oil scandal revolving around several members of his cabinet. In addition, Harding was rumored to have fathered at least one child during extramarital affairs.

But as the playground that was Chatham in the summer continued, the problems of Washington must have seemed very far away. Harold Dunbar's next-door-neighbor, Miss Josephine Atkins, entered a bean guessing contest at a fair held by the Woman's Club and won when her guess was exactly one bean off from the total of 297.

Chatham's largest real estate transfer was accomplished in August, when Roy Tomlinson, whose winter home was in Montclair, New Jersey, bought the North Chatham estate, Kinlock, of Rufus W. Page. Within two years, Tomlinson would donate the bells that Page had installed on the estate to the town. With the bells pealing every fifteen minutes, the clock on the Methodist Episcopal church tower was no longer the only timekeeper in town. Another newcomer of note was Louis D. Brandeis, whom President Woodrow Wilson had appointed to the Supreme Court in 1916. Brandeis, who was the first Jew to serve on the court, in 1924 bought twenty acres in Chatham with a small, clapboard house that he used as a family compound. The property is still held in the family and is used by Brandeis's descendants.

Throughout the '20s fads came and went. The decade began with a mah-jongg craze, and restaurants such as the Green Dragon Sea Grill opened in Chatham. When Mrs. Ralph Hopkins hosted the Rainbow Club, "Mah Jongg and chop suey gave a Chinese flavor to the evening," the *Monitor* reported on March 25, 1924. Dresses came in mah-jongg patterns and the Mayflower sold mah-jongg sets for fifty cents. By late 1924, everyone was working the new crossword puzzles, and the *Monitor* printed directions on how to solve them alongside the puzzle.

The whirligig fad had not faded, either, and Arthur Edwards was busier than ever. A check for $2.50 for a green and white windmill came from Daniel B. Giddings of the Home Trust Company in Derby, Connecticut. "We were unfortunate enough to have the one we had stolen from our veranda a short time ago." And visitors were still flocking to Shavings. "You see I enjoyed the play *Shavings* so much, that to meet the real honest-to-goodness Shavings *himself*, was a pleasure I could hardly have anticipated," L.W.C. Tuthill wrote from New York City.[89]

After Labor Day, as the cranberry season opened, Harold Dunbar entertained his mother in Chatham and Heman, Edith and Virginia Harding departed for a vacation at Lake George and Niagara Falls. The Wights returned to Baltimore, where they were living in rented rooms while Carol taught classics at Johns Hopkins University.

Men in Sheets

Unlike the membership of the early Ladies' Reading Club or the Masons, which we can recreate from documents stored at the Chatham Historical Society, the membership of Chatham's branch of the Ku Klux Klan has not come down to us.

Although Chatham remained a small town in the 1920s, immune to many of the larger issues tearing apart the nation, such as labor unrest and racial strife, it was not divorced from the world. As the Ku Klux Klan resurged nationwide during the '20s, the Cape had its own chapters. One writer speculates that a house on Harding's Beach was used "as a meeting place by the Ku Klux Klan, which was strong enough during those days to harass Catholics, Jews, and those of German ancestry."[90]

Even apart from the influence of the KKK, a vein of anti-Semitism ran through Chatham. In August 1929, when one Jewish couple entered a local inn, they saw a sign on the registration desk that read "No Dogs, No Jews."[91] Other hotels and rooming houses similarly announced in their brochures "Hebrews not accommodated" or "restricted Clientele."[92] Presumably, the hotels' guests tacitly approved of the policy; perhaps they even sought out hotels with such policies. Despite the presence of Justice Brandeis and a handful of other Jewish families, Chatham would remain for many years primarily a resort for white gentiles.

In 1923, a Chatham girl invited her Campfire Girl friends to help her celebrate her sixteenth birthday. The *Monitor* reported on February 13:

> *The table decorations were very novel, being in the form of Ku Klux Klansmen, one at every place. Most mysterious happenings took place while the guests were enjoying their spread but the dark secrets were disclosed before the end of the party, thus avoiding any possibility of nightmares to come later.*

Clearly, the teens were intrigued by the Klansmen's robes and hoods rather than their racist propaganda. That summer, the KKK float won third prize in the Fourth of July parade, "their red robes and head pieces with the comfort of corncob pipes making a clever take off," the *Monitor* reported on July 10, 1923.

But two years later, the Klan was not so innocent. Up the road about twenty-five miles in Truro, when most of the townspeople were sleeping, during what might have been a KKK initiation rite, "it happened that only a few saw the burning cross which was on the hill near the Federated church. Those who saw it were greatly alarmed," the *Monitor* reported on August

13, 1925. A week later, in Washington, D.C., Klansmen marched down Pennsylvania Avenue for nearly four hours. A local Klansman published an "open letter to the President of the Cape Cod Chamber of Commerce" in the *Monitor*, saying, "If the Klan is not needed here it's the only place in the world where it is not needed." The editor of the *Monitor* seemed to hold his nose on August 27, 1925, when he wrote, "Both sides having presented their views we respectfully request that this end the discussion so far as this paper is concerned."

In 1925, a Jewish man named Ben Shufro came to Chatham to run the Puritan Clothing Company. From the safe distance of 1982, he lightheartedly recalled his (possibly apocryphal) brush with the Klan, probably in 1925 or 1926.

One evening, Shufro told a reporter from the *Cape Cod Chronicle*, he learned where the Klan was meeting and went to the house.

> [He] *knocked loudly, not expecting an answer. When the door did open the person asked Ben, "What are you doing here? You can't come inside." To which Ben replied, "I don't want to come in, I just want to sell you your sheets."*[93]

A few months later, before the election for selectman at the annual town meeting in February, the following ominous notice appeared in the *Barnstable Patriot* from the KKK "organizer":

> *As a news item of importance to the residents of Chatham I wish to state that the Ku Klux Klan as an organization will not be in politics covering issues at the coming election in this town, or in any other town, unless conditions warrant.*

The Dunbars Break in Two

"The world broke in two in 1922 or thereabouts," novelist Willa Cather wrote.[94] Clearly the world seemed utterly different from what it had been even a decade previously. Chatham was beginning to be overrun with cars in the summer. More police were hired to maintain order. Life just wasn't as quiet as it had been.

On August 7, 1923, the *Monitor* reported:

> *Marriages are decreasing in number in Massachusetts and divorces are increasing, according to the U.S. Census bureau. In Barnstable County*

there were 218 marriages and 25 divorces in 1922, as compared with 232 marriages and 17 divorces in 1916.

Harold Dunbar hoped to add to those divorce statistics. In August 1925, two years after Brownie left him and moved into a series of rented rooms in Boston, he hired the quintessential family man Heman Harding, who lived a few houses up Main Street. Dunbar asked Harding to sue Brownie for divorce, and he arranged to pay Harding an initial legal fee of $10 by varnishing Harding's paintings of the bark *Pearl* and of Harding's grandfather. That was the only fee Harding received until November 1927, when Dunbar gave him a check for $100 against the total estimated cost of $400 or $500 for the divorce. The divorce dragged, and Harding had good reason to tire of Dunbar. Little did he know that he and Dunbar would continue their strange dance until 1933.

From almost the beginning, the Dunbar marriage had foundered. The marriage was, at the time, considered "mixed," as Brownie was a Polish Jew who had emigrated with her family in 1891. "She and her folks are Jews, never seen her father but once, as I was not allowed to come to [their] house. They thought it a sin for her to marry me," wrote Dunbar, whose religion was listed in *Who's Who in Massachusetts* in 1940 as "Swedenborgian."[95]

Brownie's family considered her strange and dubbed her "the family curio."[96] It is tempting to think that Brownie's family might not have been comfortable with her more emancipated turns. Then again, she seemed, at times, to suffer from paranoia and could be quick to pick fights when she thought someone had wronged her.

"Jan 25, 1923 I at work in studio (quiet and concentration necessary). She could see over screen, stood on chair vituperating, accusing. I warned her," Dunbar wrote in a telegraphic-style note, furnishing background information to Harding. "She did so more. I threw palette and brushes on floor. I took hold of her to stop she struck me in eye."

Added to this were the couple's financial problems. Their sole source of income was Dunbar's art. Brownie tried to peddle Dunbar's paintings through the Vose Gallery in Boston, but they sold slowly. Meanwhile, Dunbar made a few dollars through his art classes.

And finally, darker, more intimate troubles rumbled beneath the surface. Dunbar wrote to Harding:

Our married life was happy enough, except for the fact that she refused from the first my natural advances, giving reasons of illness in excuse. Later,

> *when we were financially worried, she refused because she felt we could not afford the expense of children. When she finally ceased this opposition, our sexual relations were not satisfactory, owing to something which I thought to be a physical defect in her, but owing to my lack of experience with women, did not understand.*

Dunbar's portrait of Brownie, painted in Paris in 1914 on their wedding trip, shows a handsome woman with heavy eyelids, a long nose and full lips. She wears a string of pearls around her neck. The pinkish flesh tones of her face glow inside the dark corona of her hat and jacket. She is posed in the classic three-quarters position of the *Mona Lisa* (which, interestingly, had just been returned to the Louvre in 1913, while the Dunbars were in Paris, after having been stolen in 1911).

During the summer of 1924, Dunbar's second summer in Chatham as a bachelor, he began publishing a series of essays in the *Monitor*, the *Hyannis Patriot* and other local papers. Written in purple prose, they reveal Dunbar's attitude toward his new hometown—and further, since many of his readers would have been summer visitors, he helps to propagate the myth of Chatham as the quintessential small town.

He praises Chatham as a place without burglaries, where peace and quiet prevail. In July 1924, obviously turning a blind eye to the mobs who showed up to celebrate the Fourth, he wrote:

> *It is a very comfortable feeling to stroll down the street, hearing the ocean not far away and the birds all about, getting glimpses of cranberry bogs, sand hills and salt bays, recognizing most of the few people you meet and feeling absolutely careless about whether you happen to have on a necktie or not.*

He finally compares Chatham to heaven. At the end of the day, when "the moon glitters on the quiet sea and the whispering surf breathes of mysterious distances, we become filled with a tranquil faith that in the end 'All's well.'"

"The sea is our heritage," he writes in August. Yet in the next sentence, he marries Chatham's shoreline to tourists, not fish: "People come from all over America to play in our back-yard. It has been, and will always be, our fortune and our best asset." In late August, he writes a paean to the Chatham oyster that must have sent many a casual visitor reeling "down the hill to the little shanties by the river," where "genial oyster-men" would be glad to open some of those "succulent bivalves." "Eat them there," he advises, "where the salt breeze blows and the gulls circle overhead."

Brownie Dunbar, painted in a classic pose by her husband Harold on their 1914 honeymoon in Paris. Ten years later, the marriage foundered as Brownie "went mad" and Harold sought a divorce. After Harold's death in 1953, many of his paintings and sketches were retrieved from the town dump. *Photo by the author from a painting at the Chatham, Massachusetts Historical Society.*

Benign as the summer ocean may have appeared, the waters off Chatham remained as treacherous as ever. In August, Dunbar recounted the sinking of the six-masted schooner *Wyoming*, which had been riding out a storm off Chatham the previous March. "It was a furious night," he wrote, and his words must have thrilled many a summer visitor curling their toes in the warm beach sand of August. "The storm roared, and the village houses trembled. By morning the sea was chaotic, a wild mass of driving foam. The rain blew horizontally, as if shot from a fire hose." On the second night, "the street lights were out, I could not see my hand against the sky," he continued. "The surf pounded like the roar of artillery along a fifty-mile front." And finally, the *Wyoming*, its crew of fourteen and its coal "vanished into the sea's great mystery."

In October, Dunbar published a sentimental piece about a marvelous old woman he knew. In it, Dunbar, who had now been living apart from his wife for over a year and a half, outlines his idea of the perfect wife for an artist. She would be content to live "in a quiet village," and her duties to her husband would be "to care for him forever."

Brownie Goes Mad

During the first of many interviews with Heman Harding, Harding asked Dunbar to write a description of his marriage. Dunbar wrote:

> *After she left me, I suffered keenly from loneliness and discouragement, I lost all ambition, gave up my career as I had formerly planned it, and retired to this village on Cape Cod. I have made no friends, acquired no property, and have indulged in no extravagances.*

Finally, in words that must have made Harding raise his eyebrows, Dunbar, a man whom those who knew him usually described as "colorful," added, "I live as simply as possible, mind my own business, and ask nothing from the world but a chance to paint the interesting things I see every day about me."

While Dunbar had originally thought to sue Brownie on the grounds of "cruel and abusive treatment," to "spare" her he agreed to Harding's suggestion that he sue Brownie for desertion.

During the summer of 1926, the burning issue seemed to be how much alimony Dunbar, who was now living full time in Chatham, might be able to provide. Heman Harding and an ever-changing cast of attorneys

Back in 1920s and '30s, fishing shacks at the end of Barn Hill Road were a favorite subject for Harold Dunbar and other painters. These are a modern-day version of the old shacks. *Photo by the author.*

representing Brownie dickered. In June, Harding wrote to Judge Harry B. Davis, "I am quite sure from what my client has told me that he could not pay more than the amount I suggested to you." And then he added, in a wry aside, "Artists, you know, are temperamental, impecunious people."

Like many others in the '20s, Dunbar had been dabbling in the bull stock market, and he said that he had lost money well before the crash. "I had nothing whatever of any value except some furniture, a second-hand Ford, a home-made radio-set, and my pictures, which nobody wanted to buy," he wrote. By November 1924, he was sending nothing at all to Brownie, who was being supported by her family. To her sister Ethel, Dunbar wrote:

> *I have at this moment, only about fifteen dollars between me and starvation, and while I am doing some work that I hope will bring me more, it is uncertain, and I am greatly worried, and cannot possibly send you any money at present.*

Yet Dunbar, ever resourceful, knew how to jump on a fad. As the world reeled on in its crazy way, a vogue for all things antique was taking hold. About a quarter mile down the road from Dunbar, the Old Harbor Antique Shop opened its doors, and its owner, Louise Driscoll, took out an ad in the *Monitor* for "high grade antiques at an honorable price." Dunbar, too, decided to make a buck from antiques and sold whatever antiques he could acquire from his Main Street home. "It has been said jokingly that there are as many Antique shops on the Cape as there are hot dog stands!" wrote Huldah Wellington Spaulding, who moved to Chatham in 1924 and wrote the book *Intimate Incidents of an Antique Shop.*[97]

By July, the rambler roses were coming late into bloom in Chatham. "Native vegetables are coming into the market quite freely now. Gardens are later than usual but are looking especially good," the *Monitor* reported on July 14. That week, Dunbar entertained Mr. and Mrs. Capri. Chatham was ever so quaint.

"If they had a place like it on the west coast its land would sell on the square inch basis," summer resident Fred L. Whalen wrote to his friend "old topper" while driving up the West Coast in August.[98]

Also in August, Harding addressed the historical society on the topic of volunteers salvaging lives and cargoes from stranded vessels. Models paraded around in historical bonnets, shawls and hoop skirts.

A wild storm caught people on the beaches. Lightning struck the tower of the railroad station and entered right into the ticket office, but no one was harmed. The summer ended, the summer people went home and the fall began as usual.

On September 18, 1926, Joseph Lincoln ordered breakfast for one in his room at the Sunset Hill House in New Hampshire's White Mountains. At Sunset Hill House, the food suited Lincoln just fine.

In pencil (of course) on the green breakfast chit, Lincoln wrote, "1 Orange Juice, 1 Canteloupe [*sic*], 1 Calves Liver & Bacon, 1 Poached Eggs, 1 Toast, 1 Coffee." He signed the chit "Jos. C. Lincoln" and penciled in his room number, 182.[99]

A wrinkle came in the Dunbar divorce proceedings. Brownie's personality tics, which had formerly won her the epithet "the family curio," apparently intensified. Now, at the age of forty-two, many of Brownie's phobias seemed to revolve around the new technology. She believed that a Dictaphone was lodged in the tree outside her home in Belmont and that she was receiving electric shocks through her bed. She was convinced that cars on the streets of Boston squirted poison onto her to inoculate her with disease. She also believed that "mysterious persons" were stalking her and stealing her clothes and papers, according to Dunbar.

Josephine Atkins, who was working on an advanced degree at Boston University's Divinity School, ran into Brownie in the Boston Public Library one day in February 1926, not having seen her in Chatham since July 1924 when Miss Atkins's guardian, Almena Kent, was dying. (Dunbar told Heman Harding that Brownie had refused to stay with him during that visit, which lasted for a few days.)

Atkins noticed nothing odd about Brownie. Yet by the end of 1926, Brownie had apparently become "mad." The Brownsteins committed her, in the new year, to a Boston psychiatric hospital. From there, she moved to the Brattleboro Retreat in Brattleboro, Vermont. Her father, Bernard W. Brownstein, was duly appointed as guardian ad litem. The case dragged on.

"I have never seen an insane person, and do not know who may or may not be called sane," Dunbar told Harding. He said that he attributed Brownie's "mental peculiarities" to a fever she had as a child. He added that he "thought of her illusions as a sort of mental scar, from which she would eventually recover, as in every other way she had an unusually keen intellect, and I thought her a remarkably able and attractive personality." In all of Dunbar's existing writings, this is probably the highest praise he grants Brownie.

Meanwhile, Dunbar's public persona continued at odds with his private one. In a *Hyannis Patriot* article titled "No News," Dunbar dubbed himself the "town idiot" who

> *paid his bills last month about as usual, though his income since Thanksgiving amounts to $2.37. This was because when the fish bit last summer, he pickled them. If business keeps up like this, he hopes to get pickled himself.*

In June, the newspapers were full of Charles Lindbergh, who flew solo to Paris and stepped out of his plane a hero. During his flight, the RCA station—what had been, before the war, the Marconi station in Chatham—was in contact with Lindbergh. The station now operated under the call letters WCC (Wireless Cape Cod) and specialized in ship-to-shore communication in Morse code.

In late November, Dunbar appeared in court; the Brownsteins planned to fight the divorce. Meanwhile, Dunbar was getting frantic and considering heading out to Nevada for a divorce.

The day after celebrating his own wedding anniversary, Harding wrote to discourage Dunbar from going to Nevada. "Illness and the upset of my office has prevented me from answering earlier," he added.

Dunbar said that he was loathe to return to court. "After it was over, I should be no better off, certainly, than now, and should still be obliged to go to Nevada, and I am nearer Nevada by 800 miles right now," he wrote from Ohio. He added that his November court appearance was so repugnant to him that "I would rather commit suicide than go through it again."

On Leap Day, Harding encouraged Dunbar to return to Chatham to wrap up matters. "Your letters seem to indicate that you misunderstand some things I write you," he chided him. "I do not know whether that is my fault or yours, but it is very unsatisfactory trying to handle as important a matter as this through letters."

On March 5, Dunbar wrote from the Auditorium Hotel in Chicago that he would come back to Chatham. "I realize that it is unsatisfactory for me to have been away at this time, but if I had remained in Chatham, I should be utterly broke by now, and I am lucky to have had some work this winter."

Just before Memorial Day weekend, Dunbar was once again back in Barnstable County Court. A pile of medical and legal evidence attested to Brownie's insanity. For a few days, Dunbar had to sit tight while Judge Collen C. Campbell of the Probate Court at Barnstable pondered his decision in *Dunbar v. Dunbar*.

Life continued. The "van guard of the summer people" were rolling into town, the *Monitor* noted on June 21, 1928. The best place to observe them was at the post office when the evening mail arrived off the train. Sunday mail service was now beginning with the lobby open from 11:30 a.m. to 8:00 p.m. In addition, yachts and speedboats "of all colors and sizes" dotted the Mill Pond.

Finally, on June 20, Campbell issued his ruling in *Dunbar v. Dunbar*: divorce denied. Because Brownie was affected by "lunacy," she could not entertain a "conscious volition" to desert Dunbar. "Therefore IT IS DECREED that said libel be dismissed without prejudice." Dunbar remained a married man.

The parties wrangled for the rest of the summer over how much, if any, alimony and support Dunbar should pay Brownie. Harding was unwell as the fall began. "I have been getting very tired through the summer, finally got an attack of what was probably the grippe, and for the last ten days have had a recurrence of my old trouble, so that I have been in my office but once," he wrote on September 28.

Talking pictures came that winter. "It takes a little time to become accustomed to the voices but after looking and listening to the combination a plain picture without sound will seem probably lifeless," the *Monitor* noted in January.

Still, Dunbar toyed with the idea of a Nevada divorce until a "prominent attorney" told him that Nevada divorces were invalid in Massachusetts.

And Dunbar wanted to come back to Chatham. He wrote to Harding, "The trouble is that one gets attached to a place, like a cat, and hates to go anywhere else."

The Carnival of Life

In Chatham, the summer carnival was on, with "strange faces" seen more frequently than familiar ones, the *Monitor* reported on July 4, 1929. A James Elwood came in from Detroit to retrieve the remains of his father, who died in the Hawthorne Inn of pneumonia. "He was advanced in years but had anticipated his visit here, thinking it would be a tonic," the *Monitor* reported.

The summer of 1929 was a drought summer, with the possibility of fires increasing in the dry brush. In late July, a wienie roast got out of control and lit beach grass. A man named Ronald Archibald, while loading a cigarette lighter, accidentally ignited the lighter fluid and burned both hands.

Helen W. Powell, her sister and three friends, on a trip from Landsdowne, Pennsylvania, passed through Chatham on their way to Maine. While they were in Chatham, Arthur Edwards fastened a little windmill onto the radiator of their car. When, after a trip to New York City, they discovered that the little windmill was gone, "Well, we thought we had lost a friend," Mrs. Powell wrote. "It was as tragic a loss, at any rate." She enclosed one dollar for a new one.

Fat Mrs. Gulick of Worcester sent Edwards a photo of the two of them that she was "more than proud of." Also in the photo was a stranger. "The young lady with the hat, we do not know," she wrote, adding, "Mr. Gulick had her step into the picture."

In August, a seaplane parked by Oyster Pond began taking people up for rides over Chatham. Wilfred Berube, a French Canadian chauffeur to the summer people the Shattucks, had learned to fly. Soon, Berube, almost single-handedly, built Chatham's airport. The first thunder storm of the summer came in mid-August and was followed by fog. In any case, the end of the drought came too late for the summer corn, which was stunted. Fred Wight displayed an oil painting of Charles A. Howes called *The Sailmaker* at Chatham Bars Inn.

By the end of the '20s, Chatham was paying a price for its popularity. In 1929, Chief Eldredge reported in his year-end summation that he drove his own car twenty-four thousand miles, and he believed it was time for the town to finance a police car. He wanted an extra officer for the busy summer months, and he also wanted a police emergency signal. A flashing light on one of the church steeples or one blast of the fire whistle would serve. Under the current system, he had to telephone various Main Street stores to locate his police officer. "This method works very good during the time the stores are open, but after closing time we have no way of being notified when we are wanted," he noted.

That year the department recovered stolen property, including one automobile, an outboard motor, a bicycle, a clock, a mahogany sea sled, three razors, a pair of rubber boots, a pair of trousers, a quantity of canned goods, cigarettes and candy, household furniture, pillows, cots and blankets, silverware and cooking utensils.

Among the more serious cases the department investigated were two cases of assault and battery, one assault with intent to commit rape, five cases of breaking and entering, six liquor law violations and five drunks. There were twenty-three motor vehicle violations.

And in the background, communicable diseases had still not gone away. In Chatham, the Board of Health reported two cases of tuberculosis, three cases of scarlet fever, eighteen cases of measles and one case of chicken pox in 1929. More horribly came one case of smallpox—caught by a resident of an unnamed Cape town from someone in Middletown, where there had been an outbreak. The case was promptly quarantined.

"This was very fortunate indeed, as a few cases of smallpox in the County at this particular time would have very seriously hurt or ruined what was perhaps the most prosperous Summer the Cape has ever had," A.P. Goff, MD, of the county Board of Health wrote in the 1929 town annual report.

In August, Flo Lewis, "the red head who first put the tousled head, skimpy-skirted flapper into the spotlight," opened in Al Johnson's *Bib Boy*. An ad for Chevrolet showed an open peacock, "Announcing a Variety of Colors on the Chevrolet Six at no extra cost."

Six years after one of the Twin Lights had been moved to Nauset, bewildered visitors were still asking where it was. If that wasn't bad enough, now a For Sale sign had sprouted on the Old Mill, dated to 1797, overlooking the pond. Charles Hardy, the developer of Chatham Bars Inn, had bought the mill property in 1908. Mr. Hardy repaired the mill so that it was once again grinding corn, and although the mill was fraught with accidents, a severe storm in August 1929 finally wrecked the trundle and arms. Also, the mill had become a favorite with people bearing jackknives who had fixations on their own initials.

"It seems time to take immediate steps to save this, so far as we know, the only mill on Cape Cod in its original and so conspicuous a position," a

The Old Mill, dating from 1797, once stood on a bluff overlooking the Mill Pond. Harold Dunbar and other painters obsessively painted the mill. When the mill was threatened with demolition in the 1920s, Dunbar championed its preservation. *Photo by the author.*

"Citizen and a Subscriber" to the *Monitor* wrote in August. The loss of the Twin Light was horrible, but the loss of the mill would be just too much. Yet obstacles to preserving the Old Mill were too great, until 1954, when the mill was declared a historical landmark and moved to Chase Park.

And so the "most prosperous Summer" turned into fall. Over Labor Day, the heat was "extreme" and traffic on the Cape's roads "fearful," the *Monitor* observed on September 5, 1929. At the same time, Joseph Lincoln addressed the semiannual meeting of the historical society and recalled incidents, "which served also as he related them to remind of the many changes which had taken place in the manners and occupation of the people."

As the *Monitor* noted on October 17, "Probably the greatest factors in the transformation of the Cape are the automobile and the important highways." Four days earlier, on a misty Sunday evening, a prominent Barnstable man had driven off the drawbridge into the Cape Cod canal. The man, Milton L. Baxter, and his car, a Graham-Paige, seemed to disappear into thin air. "In the meantime the bridge was closed to traffic and hundreds of autos choked the roads in one of the worst traffic jams ever seen on the Cape road," the *Monitor* reported on page one on October 17. Clearly, two drawbridges connecting Cape Cod with the mainland were no longer sufficient.

In late October, over the course of three days, the bottom fell out of the stock market and millions of Americans were ruined overnight. Yet the *Monitor* ignored this event. The annual chicken pie supper was to be held in the vestry of the Methodist Episcopal church. The high school senior class, anticipating its springtime trip to Washington, was making fudge to raise money for the trip. A taxpayer asked for "permanent sidewalks. We have long enough been expending for roads to please autoists." And on November 5, Jim Cardozo of Chatham advertised in the *Monitor* for a phonograph motor and a pair of pants he had lost on Harwich Road under circumstances not made explicit.

On November 20, Charles Ashley Hardy, the man who had spearheaded the building of Chatham Bars Inn fifteen years earlier and who only that year was so instrumental in getting Eastward, Ho! on its feet, died in a shooting accident on his fifty-fifth birthday. Some suggested that his death was related to his recent losses in the stock market.

A few days after the stock market crashed in October, the Reverend Carter of the Methodist Episcopal Church had given a sermon deploring "the evident materialism of the present day world, its harvest being surely atheism," as the *Monitor* reported.

Perhaps the good reverend might have saved his breath. Within a short time, the world was to change again, leaving behind the fun and frivolity of the '20s.

In early December, a strange scene would have greeted anyone peering at the view from Chatham Light. Unusually high tides joined forces with ten-foot waves to prevent Coast Guard personnel from reaching the station as their car was marooned in the waves. Reverting to the technology of a decade or more earlier, someone dispatched a horse and wagon into the waves to rescue the car. The horse and wagon fared no better than the car, the *Monitor* reported.

Harold Dunbar, alone with his cat in his cottage near the ocean, ended the decade as he had begun it—a married man. On December 31, after supper (let's say canned beans because Dunbar was fond of beans), perhaps he lit a pipe, whisked Captain Kidd from a comfortable chair, rested his feet on the rusty stove rail, picked up a newspaper and turned on the radio. And as the Jazz Age gave way to the Great Depression, perhaps he listened to Schubert's Unfinished Symphony "while the boom of the surf in the black night intensified the mystery and power of that epic of cosmic forces."

BROTHER, CAN YOU SPARE A DIME?

Once I built a railroad, I made it run, made it race against time.
Once I built a railroad; now it's done. Brother, can you spare a dime?

—Yip Harburg, 1931

Something of Her Past

"We returned to Chatham year round, but not to the desperate life we had known," Alice Stallknecht Wight wrote toward the end of her unpublished memoir *Something of My Past.*[100]

> *I am not going into it, but one difference, I was painting, and the excitement, the turmoil, was now there. I had tried to come close to these people around us, but now it seemed to me that I came closer painting them, as though I had learned how.*

At the start of the Great Depression in 1930, Alice was again living in the house at the end of Stage Harbor Road in Chatham. With her were her husband Carol and, occasionally, their son Fred, who at twenty-eight was already beginning to make a name for himself as a painter.

Chatham was a very different town than it had been when the Wights first arrived on a hot Sunday in August 1910. Many of the dirt roads had been paved and the town had been electrified. Water mains were being dug. And, most importantly, the summer visitor was vital. "We must all admit that without this great industry—the entertainment of our summer population—we would be in a serious state of affairs," a June 1930 newspaper article headlined "Ten Commandments for Cape Cod" preached.[101] Alice,

Alice Stallknecht Wight's house at the end of Stage Harbor Road today. The Wights bought the property, then a derelict farm, in 1910. The house, where residents posed for Stallknecht's murals, has been modified since Stallknecht's death in 1973. *Photo by the author.*

who was planning her first mural, *Christ Preaching to the Multitude*, would unintentionally do her part for the summer trade. The mural would place her, and the town of Chatham, on the national stage and bring ever more sightseers. Alice would be, for a time, famous.

Alice was born in New York City on March 4, 1880, the third of four daughters of Frederick and Grace Platt Stallknecht. She grew up in a "hideous" Victorian house in Orange, New Jersey, amid an eccentric collection of relatives tended by Irish servants.

Much of what we know of Alice Stallknecht's intimate life comes from *Something of My Past*, which she finished writing after Carol's death. By turns extremely frank and elusive, the memoir must be treated with caution as a source. While Alice has changed many names, other names are real. On occasion, the memoir reads as though Alice is settling old scores. After Alice's death, her son Frederick (nicknamed Fritz and, later, Fred), himself a novelist, a painter and eventually a professor of art and director of the University of California at Los Angeles Art Galleries, annotated the memoir with his own thoughts and recollections.

In 1901, Alice married Carol Van Buren Wight, and by way of preparation for the marriage, Alice's mother gave the naive young woman a pornographic novel. Fred was born in 1902, and then, Alice writes, "Carol came home from New York and out of the clear air—the winter night air—he tried to kill me."

Carol, whose behavior had been erratic for some time, armed himself with a carving knife and tried to choke Alice, according to *Something of My Past*. At the turn of the twentieth century, the field of psychiatry was in its infancy. It seems probable that today Carol would be diagnosed and treated with appropriate medications. Lacking pharmaceuticals, doctors initially recommended that Carol engage in manual labor. For many years after his breakdown, the small family shuffled between New York and a changing rural scene as Carol tried to regain equanimity while working on various farms.

On that Sunday in 1910, Alice, Carol and young Fred had been the only passengers to step from the train into Chatham's turreted Victorian railroad station. The Wights thought that they might start over as farmers in Chatham, where they knew not a soul.

"When we left the train we were at the end of the line in every sense," Alice wrote about the family's arrival. A "barge"—a kind of stagecoach—picked up the family and its luggage. "We entered from the rear or stern into darkness, and could just see out through chinks. The little old man who was driving us had a red wig with white hair curling out from under it." (Joshua Nickerson II identifies this person as Parker Nickerson, who, he confirms, covered his bald head with a gray wig on weekdays and a red wig on Sundays and holidays.)[102] It is clear that Alice is tired and no doubt apprehensive about the future among strangers in this unfamiliar backwater.

The coach driver dumped the family and its luggage in front of the Eldredge Public Library—although Alice fails to mention the library, an imposing brick building partially enveloped in ivy. Across the street was the white Methodist Episcopal church, with the four-faced town clock in its steeple.

"The [church] doors were open and the congregation was coming out on a blast of guttural organ music," Alice writes. Alice describes the staring congregation "all in dense black…They took us in without change of expression as though we were weeds that had sprung up on the lawn overnight."

Alice instructed Carol to inquire into the location of Pleasant House, the name she gives the nearby boardinghouse where they would stay until November, when legal matters were settled on their new house on Stage

Harbor Road. "We walked while the organ still played; it might have been a wedding march for our new life," she writes. The family's early days in town were rough—first, she says, a neighbor tried to sell them a dry cow, and then, when they obtained a milk-producing cow, no one would buy the milk so they had to give it away.

After nearly a decade in Chatham, in 1919 the Wights moved to Baltimore so that Carol could resume his studies in classics at Johns Hopkins University. Although they sold their farm animals, they kept their Stage Harbor house for vacations and summers. After completing his BA at the age of thirty-nine and earning his MA and PhD in the space of three years, Carol then taught for six years at Johns Hopkins.[103] In 1929, after Carol retired, when Alice and Carol returned to Chatham, Alice began her great period of painting.

The 1930 census report lists Carol's occupation as retired and Fred's as a painter of portraits. Under Alice's occupation is scrawled the word "none."

As she began planning *Christ Preaching to the Multitude*, Alice found her models in the pews of the First Congregational Church of Chatham. The church, set on a low hill overlooking Main Street, dated back to 1720, when the town's founder, William Nickerson, led services. In the 1930s, the church, now in its third location, remained prominent in the town's social life, despite competition from the Methodist Episcopalian and Universalist churches up the street. The Holy Redeemer Church was built a couple of blocks off Main Street in 1915.

As 1930 began, a small spruce outside the church twinkled with fifty Christmas lights. Church officials took turns switching the lights on and off each evening. The week before, Santa had visited the tree, and "a very jolly fellow he proved to be," Alice Guild wrote in the *Monitor* on January 2, 1930.

The big excitement as the decade began was that the Orpheum Theatre was closed to be outfitted with the new Western Electric sound system. "The acoustic qualities will be perfect due in no small measure to the experiments which Manager [Theodore] Bearse has made," Alice Guild wrote in her *Monitor* column of January 25. When the theatre opened in February with the pre-release of *Charming Rainbows*, "the lining of the walls with celotex [was] a great help to the new machine in producing pleasing tones."

Less pleasantly, diphtheria lurked on the horizon—young Frances Edwards and "little Geraldine Bearse" of South Chatham had both fallen ill. "Dr. Goff made early inspections and thought there was no reason to fear an epidemic," Alice Guild wrote on January 16, but by the end of the month, schools had been closed for eleven days. Nineteen children were afflicted. When schools reopened at the end of the month, attendance was

The First Congregational Church of Chatham, known as "the little church on the hill," circa 1930. Alice Stallknecht's first mural, *Christ Preaching to the Multitude*, was mounted just inside the big double front doors in 1932. *Photo courtesy of the Chatham, Massachusetts Historical Society*.

about half of what it should have been, but gradually the children came back to school as their parents' fears waned.

Water flowed under the streets through the newly laid water mains "and is now available for domestic use where ever house connections have been made," the *Monitor* reported. "A force of men is kept busy making new connections and are especially fortunate in having no snow to contend with and very little freezing weather so that trenches can be made easily." The new town building, which housed the high school and town offices, would soon be connected.

At the historical society's winter meeting, Alice Guild was elected president and Heman Harding was elected to the board of directors. Old laces and pipes were the subjects of talks. One speaker said that "he thought the ladies of today smoked more gracefully than the granddames of his boyhood."

The Cape Cod Gas Company placed an article in the town warrant to petition to lay gas mains in the streets. It was estimated that gas would come to Chatham in 1932. The first day of the town meeting in February moved along swiftly, but the second day "developed some oratory, sometimes getting quite warm but never developing into a good town meeting scrap," Guild reported on February 6.

In late February, "Bluebirds, quite a sizeable flock of them, were reported as visiting the yard of Miss Cora Smith of Chathamport," Guild reported on February 20. But hopes of an early spring were dashed by a terrible blizzard, the first one bad enough to stop an Acme Laundry truck from going about its rounds delivering and picking up laundry.

The Cape Cod Chamber of Commerce, founded in 1921, now boasted forty-five members from Chatham, including Heman Harding (who served as vice-president), Joseph Lincoln, Joshua Nickerson II, William C. Smith and Roy Tomlinson. Locally, the Chatham Board of Trade printed ten thousand copies of a map of Chatham, emphasizing its historical points. The board clubrooms would be staffed for ten weeks during the summer season, with a "comfort station" available.

Josephine Atkins had plunged into her theological studies at Boston University but came home for a midwinter vacation. In March, resident Kate Gould died and left her property in the center of Main Street, alongside the Wayside Inn, to the Town of Chatham. After protracted legal wrangling, the town, which first declined the land and compelled the library to take over its upkeep, eventually named a park after Gould. The Chatham Band, formed in 1931, later performed in a bandstand in the park.

And now Alice Stallknecht was inviting the people of the Congregational Church to her home to sit for her. One by one they posed: Mary Hardy and her nearly deaf daughter, Edna, the librarian at the Eldredge Public Library; and six members of the Eldredge family, including the two deacons seated in the dory behind Christ and little James W. Eldredge Jr., then a baby in diapers. William Smith's wife, Florence, posed and so did one Nickerson, three Atwoods and a Bearse, thirty adults and children in all.

Once the model was seated, Alice would quickly sketch him or her in charcoal. "The subject made her a present of one hour, no more and no less; in this land time is money," Fred writes. "By then the head was done, and the hands well along, with the rest of the figure laid on either with lines of charcoal or black paint."

Only after the subject had gone home would Alice finish the painting. "I wish I could convey the intensity of the painter at work," Fred writes. "The paint flew, and much of it lit at random, over the floor and of course over herself." Draped in a large apron, and with a palette across her knees, Alice worked with one brush in hand and two or three others in her mouth "so that a broad grin of paint would soon extend over her cheeks. She was also continually putting a point on a loaded brush with her lips, a practice not to be recommended," Fred adds. During the lean years of the Depression, Alice was said to economize by using house paint.

Alice's inspiration came from the Gospel of Matthew: "And great Multitudes were gathered together unto him, so that he went into a ship, and sat; and the whole multitude stood on the shore."

The strength of the triptych lay in its composition, with rows of people arrayed to the right and left of the dory, in which Christ stands in the bow looking directly out into the eyes of the viewer. Skinny Christ is beardless, wearing belted trousers, with his right hand raised toward heaven and his left hand lowered as though in a blessing. In the upper left corner of the painting, Chatham Light, with its obelisk monument next to it, firmly places the event in Chatham.

Who posed for Christ? Alice never named him; she claimed he was a "composite," and the newspaper reporters believed her. Yet every day Christ, aka "Slim" Hutchings, could be seen at his North Chatham garage, pumping gas. Tall, thin, hollow cheeked—Slim had a distinctive physique.

Sabin Artemus Hutchings was born on May 17, 1893, in Penobscot, Maine. He served in the U.S. Navy in World War I and arrived in Chatham in about 1922 to work at the radio station WCC in the Marconi building. When Alice painted him as Christ for the first time, he was not yet forty and had been running his North Chatham gas station, "Slim Hutchings's Garage—Wreck and Ruin—Poverty Flat," for about three years.

Slim posed as Christ at least three times. Or rather, the first time he sat for Alice, perhaps he didn't know to what use she would put his likeness. But the second and particularly third times, Slim must have known definitely that he was Christ. Yet for decades the mystery as to the identity of Christ lingered. Even as late as the 1970s a newspaper headline declared that the Christ figure had only now been revealed.[104] Reggie Nickerson, who was born in Chatham in 1926 and is one of a handful of Alice's subjects still alive, says that everyone in Chatham knew from the start that the model for Christ was Slim Hutchings. (People who knew Slim say that he made an unlikely Christ. In 1939 a Chatham summer resident quoted Slim as expressing a very un-Christlike sentiment in the letter column of the *New York Times*: "T'ain't for nothing that we natives, strictly among ourselves, call this here town Cheathem, for we've got two months to make enough to last us all Winter.")[105]

As Alice Stallknecht painted, the first months of 1930 wore on and gave way to spring. "Returning blackbirds are reported as being seen on Atwood

Sabin "Slim" Hutchings (left) in a World War I uniform and a friend. Slim, who ran a gas station in Poverty Flats, posed at least three times as Christ for painter Alice Stallknecht's murals. *Photo courtesy of the Chatham, Massachusetts Historical Society.*

street this week. A sure sign that it is time to begin Spring work," Alice Guild wrote in early March.

Universal toasters were on sale for ninety-five cents down and one dollar a month for four months. "Just open the door and the bread flips over," the ad reads. "Toast is always better when it's made at the table and served while it's hot." At E.B. Samson's Tenth Anniversary Sale "you can buy a boudoir lamp for as low as 98-cents." And the Acme Laundry still strove to liberate women. An "old-fashioned wash day robs you of time, energy and nervous force," the ad reads. "Hundreds of women in this community have found freedom by turning to our modern laundry service."

Joseph Lincoln's Problem

Joseph Lincoln had a problem. The cable bringing electricity to Crosstrees had been cut, and the responsible party seemed to be the Chatham Water Company, which had been digging and laying water lines outside his house on the Boulevard (which would become Shore Road in 1937).

Water lines came to Chatham about a decade later than electricity. In 1926, through an act of the state legislature, the privately held Chatham Water Company was brought into existence. Its founders included Joshua Nickerson II and Heman A. Harding. Its charter specified that it could lease and take lands and waters by eminent domain in its goal of laying pipes and aqueducts.

Before water mains were laid, all water came from backyard wells. But piping water from a central source not only meant that water service would be more reliable than in the past, but it also meant that fire protection—a major issue even after a professional fire department was established in 1918—would increase through the placement of fire hydrants throughout town. In 1928, the company outlined a plan to extend its service to the border of Harwich as long as the town contracted with the company to install twenty-five additional hydrants along the main line.

"While not distinctly promising to employ all local labor, they may give local labor preference providing the real wage is no higher," the company wrote in its bid. Just as existing houses had to be initially wired for electricity, so too houses had to have pipes installed in them, and the company published an updated booklet in 1936 regarding the rules and regulations of pipe installation. ("Consumers shall use only such fixtures as the Company shall approve; and each fixture shall be placed so as to be easily inspected.")[106]

Although Lincoln had, apparently, "plainly marked" the electrical cable, the water crews still managed to cut through it, according to Heman

Harding. Aside from inconvenience, Lincoln's electrical repair bill came to $334.64, and he wanted the Chatham Water Company to pay. When the company balked at the bill, a significant sum in 1930, Lincoln turned the mess over to Harding.[107]

The water company's Arthur J. Dewing oozes unctuousness in his letter to Chatham's most famous author while carefully sidestepping the issue of the company's culpability. He requests the electrician's bill. Two days later, after a four-way conference, the company offered to make good on exactly half of Lincoln's bill, or $167.32. Harding recommended that Lincoln snatch up the offer. After hesitating, Lincoln agreed.

As the summer of 1930 wore on, mosquitoes and how to get rid of them continued to prey on everyone's minds. Cape-wide committees were formed to supervise a massive extermination program. "The work was probably not started early enough to form much protection for these months or maybe the varmints realized that their fate is sealed and are making the most of their last meals," Alice Guild wrote in July.

That same month, Alice Guild discussed a proposal to turn Monomoy, which was connected to the mainland, into a bird sanctuary as a result of the 1929 federal migratory bird act.

"The island is owned by many different people and is used in the summer by fishermen as a camping place, many having substantial cabins where the families live for two or three months," Alice Guild wrote in the *Monitor* on July 3. "During the fall it is a favorite resort of gunners. We have never heard any discussion of it as being over-hunted. The sponsors very likely were not thinking of local habits or needs."

Since the eighteenth century, Monomoy, an eight-mile peninsula off Chatham's elbow, had been home to various communities. In the early 1800s, Whitewash Village grew up around Powder Hole, a deep natural harbor. A fishing village, Whitewash had about two hundred residents, a tavern inn and a public school. The hurricane of 1860 doomed Whitewash as a viable place to live, but in the 1930s the Monomoy Branting Club, established in 1862 for the purpose of shooting brant, a kind of goose, maintained four "shanties" near Inward Point. Many residents kept camps in the area of the Old Village, not far from Monomoy Point Light.

The lighthouse complex, which had been commissioned in 1828, included a cast-iron light tower and a wooden lightkeeper's quarters. In 1923, George S. Bearse, who owned Bearse Motor Company, a Ford and Lincoln dealership on Main Street, had bought the lighthouse when it was decommissioned and eventually restored it as a gunning camp. By the '30s, it had become a favorite gathering spot for those hunting and fishing on

Four men show off the fruits of their duck hunting expedition. The Monomoy Branting Club, established in 1862 for the purpose of shooting brant, a kind of goose, maintained four "shanties" on Monomoy. *Photo courtesy of Judith B. Llewellyn.*

A party gathers at the Monomoy Point Light, purchased and restored by auto dealer George S. Bearse after it was decommissioned in 1923. The lighthouse was a favorite gathering spot for those hunting and fishing on Monomoy during the 1930s. *Photo courtesy of Ted Whittaker.*

Monomoy. While the glass in the tower had been shot out by hunters, "the house is commodious and solidly built, and has steam heat and running water," the *Cape Cod Beacon* noted in 1937.[108] The landscape, too, had a certain lonely charm. Treeless, "in June the dunes are carpeted with poverty grass…the whole landscape becomes gold against a brilliant blue sea, with the roar of the white surf constantly to be heard."

Chatham native Edwin F. Eldredge called his memories of the childhood time he spent on Monomoy "sacred recollections."[109] In a 1954 talk at the Chatham Historical Society, Eldredge spoke bitterly about the condemnation of Monomoy by the federal government. The act "was resented by those who had reverence for this area," he said. "The loss to the town was tremendous." He noted that he devoted much futile effort during his years as a selectman to trying to persuade the government to reverse its decision.

Summer resident turned year-rounder Edwin Hills Kidder, too, vigorously protested closing Monomoy off as a bird preserve. In the late '30s, Kidder, an avid bird hunter and fisherman, served as president of the Lower Cape Surfcasters Club. "It was our own little playground down there," recalls Kidder's grandson and namesake Edwin Kidder Whittaker, born in 1939, who goes by the nickname Ted. "That was another world down there."[110]

When the Hurricane of '44 made Monomoy an island, Kidder organized about one hundred men in the Lower Cape Surfcasters Club to transport four thousand sandbags to fill in the cut-through. But it was no good—with each passing storm the ocean again severed Monomoy from the mainland. Eventually, a ferry became necessary to convey woodies and their passengers from the mainland.

Back in 1914, when their two daughters were toddlers, Edwin and Bess Kidder first came to Chatham. The Kidders were a well-to-do family in Newton Center who previously had vacationed in Falmouth. But by the time of the Great War, many of their friends back home were in the vanguard of those discovering the beauties of Chatham. The Kidders bought a piece of land on Cranberry Lane in North Chatham, overlooking Strong Island and Nickerson's Neck, which would, in three years time, be the site of the Naval Air Station. There, on a bluff with panoramic views of Pleasant Bay, the Kidders built their house, Far End, and established a summer and weekend home for their family for many years to come.

In time, Edwin would establish a gunning camp, Far Acres, on Schoolhouse Pond. Francis Kendrick took care of Edwin's flyers—ironically named geese whose wings had been clipped—which were set loose to lure wild geese in for the hunters. Good times were had at the camp, recalls Ted Whittaker. "He lived a very good life."

A road leads from Selectman Edwin Kidder's house, Far End, down into a cranberry bog. A sluice gate for controlling the water level in the bog is shown at the lower right. *Photo courtesy of Judith B. Llewellyn.*

Camp Far Acres, Selectman Edwin Kidder's hunting camp at Schoolhouse Pond. Kidder maintained a flock of flyers—geese whose wings were clipped—that were used to lure in other geese. *Photo courtesy of Ted Whittaker.*

Selectman Edwin Kidder (right) is dressed for a hunting trip on Monomoy during the 1930s. Note the 920 tires on his car for driving in sand. He stands with two unidentified friends behind George Bearse's Ford dealership on Main Street. *Photo courtesy of Ted Whittaker.*

In time, Edwin bought a twenty-two-foot boat, the *Camel*. Edwin became friendly with the town's luminaries such as Harold Brett, who frequently illustrated Joseph Lincoln's novels; Elmer Crowell, the famous decoy maker; and the painters Wendell Rogers and Harold Dunbar. While Edwin moved easily in the summer community, he also mingled with the year-round community, befriending local people such as the car dealer George Bearse. (Edwin himself was a businessman who sold tires and then, on Commonwealth Avenue in Boston, Hupmobiles.) In 1936, Edwin, who became a year-round resident of Chatham in 1933 upon his retirement, was elected to the board of selectmen and began a distinguished career of public service to the town.

Those People and Their Hotdogs

Petunias bloomed "bountifully" as the fall began, and the summer people returned to the cities in droves. In late September, two dogs turned vicious and damaged two separate buildings in their quest to kill caged rabbits inside them. And the year ended as it began, with Main Street decorated for Christmas. A star atop the Methodist Episcopal church steeple caught the eye of Alice Guild. "Against the dark sky, it seems a real visitor from the heavens poised above the bustle and hurry of the working world," she wrote in the *Monitor* of December 25, 1930.

By the early 1930s, the Cape's towns were developing an identity as a whole. The influx of tourists in automobiles had affected not just Chatham but also the entire Cape. On September 23, the *New Bedford Standard-Times* ran an article citing complaints about "the indiscriminate building of state, town and county highways which threatens to ruin the trees of lovely old villages and which leaves scars in their course across country." Other distinctly "unquaint" sites were "unsightly hotdog stands," "outlandish architecture" and even old cars rotting by the sides of the highways. The lack of trees, too, was suddenly seen as grotesque, and some called for a program of reforestation.

In September 1931, thirty civic-minded citizens met in Hyannis to discuss the Cape's changes. In addition to discussion of a mid-Cape highway, adequate bridges—not drawbridges—were called for to cross the Cape Cod Canal. "A definite program is needed to prevent this precious peninsula from falling heir to all the ills of a Coney Island type of summer resort," a newspaper said.[111] "No part of Massachusetts, it is safe to say, has changed more in the last twenty years than Cape Cod."

That same month, a letter to the editor of the *New Bedford Standard-Times*, perhaps remembering the October 1929 accident that snarled the roads on and off the Cape for hours, called the most immediate need "an adequate bridge or bridges high enough to let the shipping through without the necessity of opening the draws and thus interrupting traffic over the canal."

In Chatham, the first auto fatality was recorded. In twenty accidents, twelve people were injured. "Considering the large number of automobiles on the highways during the last year, we feel this is a record to be proud of," Chief Eldredge wrote in the 1931 town annual report.

A Final Printing of the *History*

William C. Smith had nearly finished the final volume of his four-volume history of Chatham before his death on April 12, 1932. Heman Harding was one of many who were concerned lest the history be lost. In a November

1931 letter from Harding to Edward L. Hurd, Harding said that although Smith had brought the history up to the American Revolution, Smith was unable to come up with the $300 necessary for F.B. & F.P. Goss of Hyannis, who had published the previous volumes, to publish this last one (which would run nearly to the end of the nineteenth century). "He would not like to borrow the money for this printing—he being in poor health and in rather straightened financial condition," Harding writes and then suggests some scheme of underwriting. After costs were met, "he would, of course, want to secure for himself and his family such meager financial returns as there might be upon his great outlay of time and labor."

Yet after Smith's death, work on the volume dragged. Smith had deposited his handwritten manuscript in the Chatham Trust Company's safe deposit box 4194 and given a duplicate key to Harding, telling him to take out the manuscript at any time to bring it to the publisher. In 1936, four years after Smith's death, Harding's daughter Virginia, who served as her father's legal secretary, mailed the key to attorney R.D. Birch of Newton Highlands, who was administering Smith's will.

Saying that he felt that publication of the fourth volume would be a "fitting memorial" to Smith, Birch told Virginia, in a November 1, 1936 letter, that he had turned over all publication rights to Smith's children—Ilsley, an electrical engineer, and Marjorie—"with the understanding that they should proceed to complete and publish the final volume." Eventually, Marjorie's husband, Captain Broberg, completed the work. "I am glad to say that the typing was completed some time ago and it is now being edited, so I think we can all hope to see it published in the very near future," he wrote. The Chatham Historical Society would eventually publish the fourth volume during the winter of 1947, thirty years after the third volume.

The Beardless Christ

Even during the Depression the weather could make one forget one's cares for a time, and one particular Saturday in August 1932 was a beautiful day. Advance publicity had generated excitement and spread the word that that afternoon Alice Stallknecht's mural *Christ Preaching to the Multitude* would be unveiled in a ceremony on the lawn of the Old Congregational Church. Looking ahead to the unveiling, which was to be at 4:30 p.m., Stallknecht told the paper that "the event would be an occasion of deep reverence, and she feared any sensational acceptance of her work."[112]

Historian William C. Smith (1861–1932), who, despite chronic ill health, wrote *A History of Chatham, Massachusetts* in four volumes. *Photo courtesy of the Chatham, Massachusetts Historical Society.*

The afternoon was, as it turned out, a public relations specialist's dream—if anyone had been thinking precisely that way back in 1932.

"No event of recent years has focused so much attention on the activities of Chatham as has been occasioned by the unveiling of the mural by Alice Stallknecht," Alice Guild wrote in the *Monitor* on August 11, 1932. "Every newspaper has carried a picture of the picture and has printed reports and comments until anything further seems futile." Guild noted that opinions ranged from "violent partisanship for and against" to utter indifference.

News reports of the event rippled out from Chatham and onto the national scene. Early on, much was made of the casual appearance of Christ. "Paints

Savior Beardless in a Modern Scene," reported one Boston paper a few days before the murals were hung. "Figure in Corduroy Trousers Seen in Dory Preaching to Chatham, Mass., People. 2 Deacons at the Oars."[113]

The *Boston Herald* estimated that the crowd on the lawn was made up of between three and four hundred "cosmopolitan" native and summer residents. As the drapes were removed from the mural, "the gathering paid it the supreme tribute of utter silence and rapt scrutiny." Twenty-nine in the audience were depicted in the mural themselves, the *New Bedford Standard-Times* reported on August 7, 1932, the day after the unveiling. (One wonders if Slim Hutchings, still unidentified, sat with the crowd, unknown to the newspapers.)

"I have endeavored to make the head of Christ, though human, also spiritual," Alice said.

A week later, on August 15, *Time* magazine published a piece on the mural under the headline "Holy Dory." "Engrossed mainly with fish and summer visitors, Chatham is respectable and religious," the magazine reported.

> *Most people might suppose that it would have no truck with a picture of Jesus Christ, beardless, garbed in corduroys and grey shirt without even a necktie, preaching from a dory manned by two Cape Codders. Such a supposition would be in error.*

On the contrary, the magazine noted, the Chathamites were "deeply, reverently pleased" about the mural.[114]

Appearing in the papers alongside a photo of the mural were photos of fifty-one-year-old Alice. The photos show a woman at whom you wouldn't look twice if you caught her in her yard hanging laundry or if you spied her sitting down in a church pew next to you on a Sunday morning. Plump and matronly, she sometimes wears a paisley shirtdress, sometimes a squashed hat. Her hair, which looks vaguely wavy in some photos, is pulled back from her face. She stares at the murals without the trace of an expression.

Her bland appearance is at odds with her forceful painting style, her muscular and acerbic prose and even her florid, often illegible handwriting. Why is this? Is it because through the many decades of covering over her husband's mental illness, Alice had become a master of disguise whose real self shone through only in her art?

Alice's life has often been viewed through the lens of a feminist perspective.[115] She married young, raised her son and cared for her mentally ill husband. By the time she was fifty, her son was an adult and her husband's mental state was stable. Therefore, Alice had time to devote to her art.

Frederick Wight painted his mother, Alice Stallknecht, in glamorous clothing. *Photo by the author from a painting at the Chatham, Massachusetts Historical Society.*

Yet her son Fred, in his annotations in *Something of My Past*, disagrees with this assessment. "Such an assertive expression, such an intensity, usually finds its own way out regardless of circumstances," he writes. He seems to claim that some glitch in Alice's own personality prevented her from painting earlier on.

Newspaper stories about Alice are almost invariably condescending. Aside from the common misspelling of her name as "Wright," the articles are careful to tie her in to Carol's career as a professor at Johns Hopkins—or once, incorrectly, at "Pennsylvania." The articles accord the mantle of "painter" to Fred. Alice "began painting only a year ago, having become interested in art through her son," inaccurately wrote the reporter for the *Boston Herald*.

Alice is called a "naïve" and "primitive" painter—words that suggest she is a talented amateur with no background in the arts. Perhaps it made a better story to pass Alice off as a rank beginner who hit it big with her first stab at painting.

The gene for drawing and painting, it often seems, runs in families. "My father liked to paint, and careful and cautious paintings he made," Alice writes. As an adolescent, Alice "imitated" him by copying paintings and arranging still lifes, which she then painted. "Without this my life would have been empty."

When Alice was eighteen and had graduated from high school, her father, Frederick, decided that she would attend art school in New York. In charge of the program at the School of Applied Design for Women at Seventh Avenue and Twenty-third Street was illustrator Dan Beard (later remembered as the founder of the Boy Scouts of America). "Here I drew and drew and this went on for three happy years," Alice writes. This period ended in 1901, when Alice married Carol.

In May 1932, both Fred's and Alice's work was shown in New York galleries. Again, even Alice Guild, who should have known better, assumes that Fred is the "real" painter. She treats Alice as a kind of sideshow. Alice Guild writes that Alice Stallknecht signs her work with her maiden name "to avoid any tendency of confusion with her son's reputation." Guild declines to write about Alice's paintings—she quotes at length from unnamed "critics" who say "it is not often that a woman paints with as much virility of attack" as Alice. "Her drawing is broad and bold." She chooses unfeminine subjects such as wild game. While Alice's work is "decorative, abrupt, on an heroic scale," Fred's work is "authentic," "now delicate, now bold." A subtext is that the "critics" don't know what to make of Alice's paintings because she is a woman who does not paint like a woman.

Religious subjects have been one of the great themes of western art at least since the Middle Ages. It was not unheard of for painters to add likenesses of their patrons, or even the pope, to a painting. Some commentators of the '30s attempted to square Alice with this tradition.

Mural painting, too, was in vogue during the '30s. In the middle of the decade, under Roosevelt's Works Progress Administration, artists competed for grants to paint murals in a post office or federal building in every state. While no one commissioned Alice or paid her for her work, she does fit into a larger tradition of muralists that included Diego Rivera.[116]

The church drew up a contract with Alice, voiding responsibility should the mural be damaged. The contract also specified that she would remove the mural should the church request it.

Considering the controversy that the murals ultimately engendered—the church would ask Alice to remove this one and its successor, *The Circle Supper*, in 1943—it seems a wonder that the murals were even hung at all. Through the years, a collective amnesia seemed to set in as many questioned who gave permission to hang the murals in the church. Perhaps the key lies in the young minister of the time, the twenty-three-year-old Franklin P. Cole. Cole was a "tall, good-looking man, and a very special person" with a "smart" wife, the former Eleanor Snavely. Cole was with the church for just under two years, and he was a popular preacher. "An attendance that had been small since 1900 increased by leaps and bounds—only to drop again when he left in October," a historian of the church wrote.[117]

Cole was born in the farming town of Noble, Indiana, in 1909, the eldest child of Audley and Grace Cole. At the time of his pastorship in Chatham, Cole was a student at the Boston University School of Theology. Chatham was his first church—he was not yet ordained when he served there.[118] The bulk of his career was spent in Congregational churches in Maine, with a stint serving as a chaplain during World War II. He enjoyed an illustrious career in the ministry as a writer of twelve books and a radio sermonizer. Most significantly, in his middle age, in 1966, Cole took up his own form of art—carving elm logs into folk art sculptures based on tobacco store Indians and ship's figureheads. An essay in the catalogue to Cole's 2000 exhibition at the Portland Museum of Art in Maine concludes, based on Cole's own memoir, that Cole's "first noteworthy exposure to the power of visual culture had occurred during his student ministry in Chatham, Massachusetts, in 1932" and goes on to describe Alice's murals.[119] Just as automobiles could not be viable without roads to drive them on, so Alice could not place her mural in the church without the passionate assistance of a church insider, namely the popular Cole, who would be so interested in art.

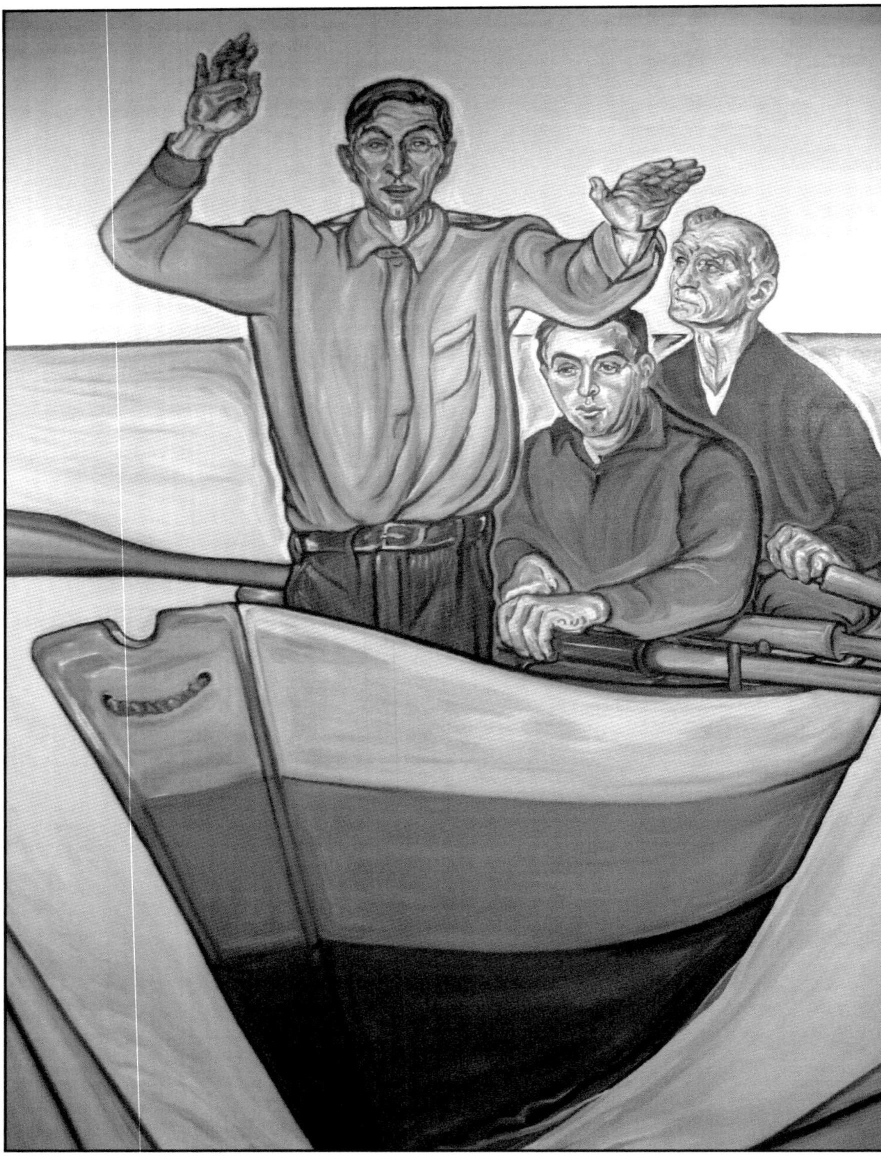

Sabin "Slim" Hutchings is depicted as a beardless, casually dressed Christ in Alice Stallknecht's *Christ Preaching to the Multitude*. Holding the oars behind Hutchings are two deacons of the First Congregational Church, both Eldredges. *Photo by the author from a painting at the Chatham, Massachusetts Historical Society.*

Cole, who was seven years younger than Alice's son Fred, vigorously supported Alice and the murals. During the dedication of *Christ Preaching to the Multitude*, the church's large white double doors were flung open, and Cole posed dramatically at the top of the steps to address the crowd below, an echo of Christ in his dory behind him addressing the multitudes.

"Here is a Christ for our age, a Christ with muscles of steel, heart of gold, and a radium like countenance," Cole said. "The artist of this magnificent mural has made Christ live again for our modern age, and this Church on the Hill owes her a debt of gratitude which our powers of expression can never make known."[120]

Cole had been "called" to the Congregational Church on January 13, 1931, at an annual salary of $1,300. He left the church on August 28, 1932, a few days after leading the dedication of the murals, to return to his theological studies at Boston University. "It is with a feeling of hesitancy and a sense of disappointment that I leave your historic and honorable pulpit," he wrote to L. Sidney Atwood, president of the Congregational Society, in his letter of resignation.[121] "I need not remind you of the happiness and satisfaction that has come both to my wife and myself during the past two years." He called his time in the church "years of contentment and joy."

During the months that followed, Cole would write letters to the editor whenever someone slammed Alice's mural in print. When the Reverend Carl A. Seaward of Swampscott wrote that "the Chatham citizens are apparently devising a means to glorify themselves by an act of defamation of the historic Christ of Palestine," Cole rebutted, saying that, in fact, Alice's models knew nothing about "the purpose, theme and destination of her mural."[122]

Cole preached at the church during the summer of 1934, and, most significantly, he returned as a "happy surprise"[123] during the summer of 1935 to attend the ceremony at which Alice's second mural, *The Circle Supper*, was dedicated.

Brother, Can You Spare a Dime?

The Great Depression was on, and by the end of 1932 Chatham was feeling pinched. The three selectmen had always borne the additional moniker "overseers of the poor," and now their burdens in that department were onerous. While in 1928 the town had expended $2,412.75 in the "support of the poor" and an additional $1,481.82 on "mother's aid," by the end of 1932 it was expending nearly $8,000.00 on relief and $6,113.25 on a new-line item: old-age support in those days before the federal Social

Members of the Hardy family and others watch and listen to Christ preaching in Alice Stallknecht's *Christ Preaching to the Multitude. Photo by the author from a painting at the Chatham, Massachusetts Historical Society.*

Security program. The "support of the poor"–line item paid for groceries and provisions, coal and wood, board and care, medical expenses, cash, electricity, clothing, transportation and rent. Throughout the 1930s, these figures would climb; eventually, the town's Board of Public Welfare would become a department with its own staff. By 1937, the board was allocating over $16,000 and distributing, through the commodities division of the Works Progress Administration, 5,868 articles of clothing, as well as over 32.4 tons of tinned meat, dry goods, eggs and fruit.[124]

While Alice Guild referred in her final column of 1932 to "these days of so-called 'depression,'" money matters engaged the minds of many. The young people in the Methodist Episcopal Church debated this question in the spring of 1931: Resolved, "That Inherited Wealth is an Advantage to Young People Beginning Their Life Work." Yea or nay?

A New Tourist Attraction

On March 4, 1933, Franklin Delano Roosevelt was inaugurated as the thirty-second president of the United States. As the Depression hit what most economists now call rock bottom, he immediately began instituting his relief plans.

And for over a year, newspaper readers had been obsessed with every mother's nightmare—the March 1, 1932 snatching of the infant of Charles Lindbergh and his young wife, Anne Morrow, from his crib. After an intensive two-month search, the infant's battered corpse was found in a grove of woods a few miles from the Lindbergh home in Hopewell, New Jersey. The hunt for the kidnappers and the subsequent trial and execution of Bruno Hauptmann would engage newspaper readers for several years to come.

On May 2, just short of the year anniversary of the discovery of the Lindbergh baby, a young girl—granddaughter of a Detroit industrialist—went missing from her school in Harwich Port, just over the line from South Chatham. It seemed that kidnapping was becoming a national sport in desperate times. The case would receive national attention in the *New York Times*. The case "has served to bring the Cape into prominence in a way that is very distasteful to the people here," a page-one writer in the *Monitor* sniffed on May 4, 1933.

Kenneth Earle Buck was the youngest of nine children. His father, Joshua E. Buck, was stationed at the U.S. Coastguard Station in Chatham. The elder Buck died when Kenneth was twelve. At about that time, the entire Buck family was struck with the deadly Spanish influenza. Yet despite hard times,

Kenneth married a Chatham woman in 1923 and settled down working for J.H. Shepard Co. Plumbers and Steamfitters in Chatham. A son was born to the young couple two years later.[125]

When the child was two, in the fall of 1927, Kenneth took a job as a private chauffeur and moved with his employer to New York City. There, a series of misfortunes dragged the family down. When the child was struck by a car and needed special care, Kenneth decided to move back to the Cape and work for his elder brother, Cyril, in a garage in West Harwich.

Prohibition was on and Cyril, whom his brother describes as a "heavy drinker" who enjoyed staging "wild parties" in his home, moved in a demimonde of bootleggers and crooks. Cyril's garage proved the ideal place to store bootlegged liquor after it was brought into South Chatham's beaches from Rum Row. In time, Cyril's garage and other sites of the kidnapping would provide perverse alternatives to more conventional tourist attractions.

The kidnapped ten-year-old girl was Peggy McMath, granddaughter of millionaire William Kales. Peggy was enticed from school and driven away in a car with a "Negro chauffeur" and what the papers called "two rough men."[126] After her disappearance, a Cape-wide manhunt began, with cars pulled almost at random off the highways and searched. A pair of girl's shoes found on a Chatham beach proved to be a futile clue. Meanwhile, a "herd of newspapermen" descended on the area.

Ultimately, it was learned that Peggy was hidden in the cellar of a vacant house next to a golf course in Harwich Port. Her kidnappers provided her with an old mattress and an overcoat; she was fed ham sandwiches, milk and cocoa. The ransom was set at $70,000.

Many years later, Kenneth provided a jumble of weird details about the handover. Perhaps as a distraction, Cyril tipped off a Harwich police officer that rumrunners were planning to drop off a load on the beach in South Chatham. Meanwhile, Peggy's father Neil, with a black hood over his head, climbed into a car with Cyril at the wheel. Peggy and Kenneth sat in the back. At the Chatham Light, the group switched places in the car, with Kenneth now donning the black hood. Peggy was returned to the McMath family after seventy hours in captivity, and the next day Kenneth received $10,000 in cash. The day after that, he was arrested.[127]

Neither the police nor a jury believed Kenneth Buck's slant on the scheme—basically that he was an innocent dupe and his brother and Neil McMath were in cahoots—and he was sent to prison for twenty-five years for his role in the kidnapping and extortion scheme. From prison, Kenneth Buck continued protesting his innocence for his role in planning and executing the kidnapping.

A Potpourri of Happenings

Life in Chatham just before the summer of 1933 continued in its prosaic way. When Leon Stevens of Highland Avenue suddenly died of a heart attack, "his quiet marriage to his housekeeper, Mrs. Ellis, a few days previously, was revealed," the *Monitor* reported. And little David Elmer Howes, age four, "stepped on a cesspool cover, tipped it up, and dropped down." He clung to the sides with his hands and dangled there until rescued by Harry Forgeron's aunt. George Small had an accident while cranking his car and received extensive bruises. Harold Dunbar's mother, Nellie, came to town with Harold's brother Carl. "After a social evening she retired as usual." The next morning she was found dead in bed, a victim of an apparent cerebral hemorrhage. And at the start of June, Kenneth Buck began smashing his head on the walls of his cell, giving "the appearance of a person suddenly gone insane." He was taken in a strait jacket to Bridgewater State Hospital.

In late July an event occurred of more import for Harold Dunbar than for anyone else—his landlady, Josephine Atkins, hired a plumber to install plumbing in his house. The equipment would include an enamel iron lavatory "complete with chromium plated trimmings," a white seat and cover, a shower and a heater to provide hot water and a cesspool in the yard to take care of waste. And all of this would be "complete and ready for use" for $328, roughly half of the price of a modest car.[128]

"Now he never uses the little house out back, that had three holes and was good enough for anybody," Harold wrote in the *Cape Cod Beacon* in March 1938 under the pseudonym "Letty the Oldtimer."

On September 6, 1933, Roosevelt's federal Public Works Administration authorized construction of three new bridges—two for autos and one for trains—spanning the Cape Cod Canal. In December, workers began laying foundations for the bridges. As far as was possible, the work was done by hand to create jobs during the Depression. The Bourne and Sagamore Bridges, as they were named, would replace drawbridges built in 1911 and 1912. The old bridges were of a cantilever draw type that had to be raised whenever ships passed through the canal.[129] It was by now impractical for both auto and ship traffic to wait for the other to pass through.

At the end of December, Prohibition ended with the repeal of the Eighteenth Amendment to the Constitution. "Let's make the Cape decent and law-abiding," wrote an editorialist in the *Monitor* on December 7, 1933. "Let's purge it of the most sinister influence that America has ever known—the bootlegger."

The following year, Chatham innkeepers and restaurateurs spent $950.00 on liquor licenses and $284.95 on wine and malt beverage licenses, according to the 1934 town annual report. "One is pretty lucky to be able to buy liquor on Cape Cod," Dunbar wrote. "It never was possible until after prohibition got everybody drinking, and it may not last very long unless citizens take it easy."[130]

Unemployment was still high, and 1934 was another bad year. Some Chatham children whose families now relied on public welfare agencies were in dire need of medical and dental care and food. Their homes were "most completely disorganized," with the mother beginning the third, or even fifth pregnancy, "overwhelmed with responsibilities and physical discomfort, a discouraged and irritable husband, children crying incessantly, all living in cluttered rooms and existing on a badly balanced diet," the Board of Health wrote in the 1934 town annual report.

Beans and Brown Bread for Supper

"On Saturday night we had baked beans and brown bread for supper," Joseph Lincoln wrote in *Cape Cod Yesterdays*, his 1935 homage to a Cape already gone by.[131]

Brown bread. It used to be a staple of old New England cooking. You mix rye and wheat flours with cornmeal, moisten with molasses and sour milk, add raisins to taste and steam in a coffee can. The result is a dark, moist, round bread. In Alice's mural *The Circle Supper*, Josephine Eldredge Stockweather, wearing white high heels and a full-length apron over her dress, carries in a large bowl of baked beans. Coastguardsman Leo Kendrick follows with coffee and a mound of brown bread. The amount of food is clearly not enough to serve the fifty seated people, and it brings to mind the passage in the Gospel of Mark in which Jesus feeds five thousand with five loaves and two fishes.

The Circle Supper, which Alice began in the mid-1930s, again provides revealing snapshots of Chatham. Slim Hutchings now sits alone in a central panel with both palms turned up in a blessing. Alice presents forty-nine seated people gazing either directly out at the viewer or toward Slim. Dr. Worthing sits with his arms folded, waiting patiently for his food. Heman, Edith and Virginia Harding gaze expectantly toward the food. Also sitting in the group are Alice Guild and dentist Minnie Buck's daughter, Josephine.

On a Saturday in August 1935, on an afternoon that must have mirrored the one three years earlier, Alice's new mural was dedicated, again before

Alice Stallknecht's *The Circle Supper* occupies a prominent position in the Chatham Historical Society's Mural Barn. The barn is a former freight car that Stallknecht bought from the defunct train station to house her murals. *Photo by the author.*

several hundred people. The Reverend Franklin Cole, who had moved on to a church in Maine "having more than ten times the membership" of Chatham's Congregational church, returned with his wife and gave the benediction. Various speakers, including one from the Phillips Memorial Gallery in Washington, D.C., explicated and praised the mural. Alice denied, in the *New Bedford Standard-Times*, that *The Circle Supper* was an attempt to depict Christ's Last Supper in modern clothing.[132]

The new mural was installed on the back wall of the church's sanctuary, in the balcony, covering over the top part of the church's two tall front windows. In normal practice, only the minister, facing it, and the choir, by turning their heads ninety degrees, could see the mural. But during the summer, visitors tended to scrutinize the local people seated in the pews next to them and then swivel their heads around to see if they could pick them out in the mural.[133]

In September, the Reverend Charles Thorp, who had succeeded Cole, wrote Alice a letter commending her on her "artistic genius" and thanking her for her generosity toward the church. He noted that in the

A photo, probably from the late 1930s, showing visitors examining Alice Stallknecht's *The Circle Supper* when it hung on the back balcony wall of the First Congregational Church of Chatham. *Photo courtesy of the First Congregational Church of Chatham.*

The sanctuary of the First Congregational Church of Chatham today. Note the tall windows in the balcony, covered by Alice Stallknecht's mural *The Circle Supper* between 1935 and 1943. *Photo by the author.*

past fifty days an astonishing 11,800 persons had visited the church to view the murals.[134]

With every news article published about Alice's murals, and every novel published by Lincoln, more visitors flocked to Chatham. As the decade wore on, the Congregational church became known as "the church of the murals." "The murals by Alice Stallknecht Wight at the Congregational Church are being visited daily by a steadily increasing number of visitors from all parts of the country," Alice Guild wrote in her column on June 24, 1937. "The church is open every day, both morning and afternoon."

Harold Dunbar published a parody of the murals in his *Cape Cod Beacon* under the title "No Religious Significance." The drawing by "Ariel"—most likely Dunbar himself—shows four homely, beefy women lined up in two rows in the church's fellowship hall.[135]

The murals remained popular. A year later, the twelve thousand summer visitors to the murals had destroyed "the beautiful old red carpet in the church," the *Monitor* reported on June 23, 1938. The Ladies Aid Society promptly replaced the carpet. Church notes reveal that free will offerings given to the church by those gazing at the murals paid for a new furnace and shingled the west roof. Alice was given a silver centerpiece "as a token of their appreciation of the financial aid received by the loan of the murals."[136]

The Old Salt's Reward

Up Old Harbor Road about half a mile from the Congregational church, Arthur Edwards continued to entertain and pose for photographs with visitors enamored with the "adorable, philosophical and kind" person of Shavings.[137] The fan letters, too, continued to roll in, some actually addressed "Dear Shavings."

"We were very happy to meet you and to see your celebrated shop and your eminent self," Maud B. Church wrote to Edwards from Providence, Rhode Island.

> *Mr. Lincoln evidently likes to write about the Cape Cod folks and, now that I have met them, I don't wonder. There is a wonderful, sincere, deep-rooted honesty and home atmosphere down there. He seems to love it and to portray it so that it attracts thinking people to the Cape.*

Church, who went home with one of Edwards's wooden red-winged blackbirds, confided that her friend, Miss Dick, "is so disappointed because of her picture with you in which you are decapitated."

More than a decade after *Shavings* appeared on Broadway, we see Edwards posing with sailors in white, ladies in cloche hats, ladies with round owl glasses and men in plus fours and spats. Sometimes he stands on the porch of the shop, sometimes in the grass, and always he holds a windmill in one hand and perhaps the hand of a little girl in the other. Edwards usually wears a straw hat or a beret. He never smiles.

In 1938, the New York, New Haven & Hartford Railroad Company photographed Edwards for a brochure to be distributed at the New York World's Fair. Edwards's likeness would make New England "so attractive that they will want to make a side trip to New England," the letter to Edwards's daughter said.[138] At age eighty-one, it seemed that the "old salt" had arrived.

Alice Guild Can't Be Everywhere (Although She Seems to Be)

Alice Rose Walker Guild had by now been writing her Chatham column in the *Chatham Monitor* since her byline began to appear sometime in the 1920s.

Far from including only social and church news and snippets such as Mrs. So-and-So was recuperating from appendicitis, Alice's column also included what we today call "hard" news—descriptions of fires and automobile accidents.

Alice Walker Guild (1876–1975) was a teacher, a founder and president of the Chatham Historical Society, a decades-long chronicler of Chatham doings in the *Chatham Monitor* and a mother of six. Originally from Belchertown, Guild helped to define Chatham. *Photo courtesy of the Chatham, Massachusetts Historical Society.*

As the years went on, Alice also interjected her own opinions as she took a proprietary interest in Chatham and the way its people comported themselves.

Alice, like so many of the influential people in Chatham, began her life elsewhere. She was born in 1876 in Belchertown, a daughter of Alvah and Abbie Stebbins Walker. She became a teacher and, in her early twenties, married the school principal, Charles A. Guild, a widower some fifteen years her senior. The death of Guild's first wife left him with four children—Alice was only twelve years older than his eldest daughter, also named Alice. Within a year of the wedding, Alice had a baby of her own, Bernard, who would be followed over the next decade with five more, including a baby who died in infancy. (The March 18, 1913 notes of the Ladies' Reading Club tersely read, "This meeting was omitted on account of recent death of Mrs. Guild's baby.")

The Guilds came to Chatham in 1910, shortly before Alice Stallknecht Wight and her family arrived. Grass was still growing down the center of Cross Street when the Guilds moved into their home near Main Street. In addition to acting as principal of Chatham High School, Charles Guild was the news and advertising agent for the *Monitor*. Accordingly, Alice took on the job of local correspondent for one of the Boston papers and also joined the staff of the *Monitor*. In her weekly column, which she sent to the *Monitor* through the mail—once it was lost in the mail—she frequently enjoined her readers to send in information. "We can't be everywhere but we want all the news," she wrote on August 5, 1926.

Alice's Chatham differs from that of Joseph Lincoln and Harold Dunbar. Nary an old salt is to be seen. The town is populated by hardworking people who are often opinionated when it comes to spending the town's money. She doesn't pay short shrift to the town's year-round population, nor does she fawn over the rich summer set. Alice Guild's Chatham is a town where people grow up, work hard and know that life is not a bowl of cherries. The old are revered and the dead are mourned. Not all progress is good—nor is it all bad. Alice's tone, through the years, is brisk and no-nonsense, although she sometimes waxes rhapsodic, particularly around Christmastime, after dark, when Christmas lights and stars seem to spark her religious nature.

Widowed, Alice lived with some of her unmarried children in a "cozy and well-preserved" pre-1840 house off Shattuck Place that had been moved from near the Twin Lights. If one visited "about the time that Mrs. Guild is baking a batch of home made bread, it just spells HOME, the real old fashioned, comfortable, warm HOME."[139] Alice, whose life was busy and full, died at the age of ninety-nine after sixty-six years in Chatham.

Harold Dunbar Cuts Loose

During the Great Depression, Harold Dunbar discovered the joys of cross-dressing. Again and again, he donned women's clothing and paraded around town for the sake of the theatre and good causes. In a 1934 play, he played the role of Mabel Jackson after the drama coach "found the Cape Cod girls too demure and shy to play the part of [a] tuff and prosperous gold digger."

"While we are not exactly effeminate," Dunbar wrote about his role in that play, "our shape is the envy of all our feminine friends." As Mabel, he wore a "slinky chiffon evening gown" in black and silver topped with a scarlet hat. He "slithered upon the stage" in high-heeled slippers.[140]

During a 1937 Safety Parade, Dunbar rode on a float "wearing a nifty old straw chapeau with a lace veil to protect her [*sic*] make-up from the setting sun." At a party for the Dramatic Guild, Dunbar modeled a "white net dress worn with a short ermine cape and a white crocheted tam." True, that evening Dunbar was not the only man in drag. His friend Wendell Rogers, the painter, and Wendell's brother Fred both wore women's housecoats and house dresses. Dunbar also played with cross-gender issues when he wrote columns in the *Cape Cod Beacon* under women's pseudonyms such as Hollyhock Blossom and Gertrude Stein Jr.

Dunbar's long-estranged wife Brownie, who had undergone a mastectomy in March 1929, died on June 10, 1930, in Boston. She was forty-five. The day after her death, she was buried in Adath Jeshurun Cemetery on Grove Street in West Roxbury. Due to mental illness, breast cancer and perhaps just plain ill luck, she had never been able to fulfill her dreams of working in an art museum. Sadly, her death certificate lists her occupation as "housework." Dunbar was now a widower, but what he thought of his new status he did not immediately record.

The following spring, long-suffering Heman Harding was still trying to wrench a final payment out of Dunbar for legal services. In his shorthand, Harding wrote, "He said had wanted [to] pay me by pictures & I hadn't answered." And then the final entry, which Harding underlined in emphatic black pencil, "Finally agreed he to pay me $150.00 more," which brought the cost of legal proceedings up to $510, including the $10 Harding credited Dunbar for varnishing those family pictures. In a final handwritten note on May 25, 1933, Harding implored Dunbar, "Won't you come in & get your papers." And that, with one party dead and the bills paid, was the end of *Dunbar v. Dunbar*.

As the decade wore on, Dunbar increasingly explored the flamboyant sides of his personality. Whether he inherited money after his mother's death

Harold Dunbar sketched a self-portrait in the guest book of his next-door neighbors on Main Street in 1945. "This is the guy who painted the picture of Pleasant Bay. With regards to his good neighbors, the Stones." *Photo courtesy of Isabel Lamberg.*

in 1933 is unclear, but several months later he purchased an abandoned toy factory owned by Judge Charles Bassett in which he intended to create an artists' colony. He remodeled the two-story barn and created a studio for himself upstairs. (For a time, Wendell Rogers, who would eventually maintain a painting studio next door to the Congregational church, slept in Dunbar's studio.)

Downstairs, Dunbar painted two large murals, one called *Map of the Land of Make-Believe* and the other a scene from *Macbeth* showing Macbeth's enemies gathering for the attack on the gloomy castle of Dunsinane.

By the late '30s, Dunbar's "Guild Hall," where he frequently took to the stage himself as a member of the Dramatic Guild, was a well-established place for the theatre and community gatherings. (In 1938, Mary Winslow of the Wheaton College Theatre Department established a young stock company in the building, which she bought from Dunbar and renamed the Monomoy Theatre.) Even during the off-seasons of the Depression, the Dramatic Guild staged plays such as *Tumble Inn*, with Dunbar playing character roles such as "Dickey," aka Richard Simpson-Sampson.[141]

Gunboat and Gunny Go Aboriginal

In January 1935, the final girder of the Sagamore Bridge, extending over the Cape Cod Canal, was riveted. The following August, thousands attended the dedication of the twin Sagamore and Bourne Bridges, which had opened to automobile traffic in June. President Roosevelt was rumored to be coming to the ceremonies, but Boston mayor James Curley came instead and gave a speech. Current estimates put the crowd watching the seven-and-a-half-mile parade between the bridges at between one and two hundred thousand.[142]

Now that the two bridges were in place, the next thing the Cape needed was a mid-Cape highway that would travel along the Cape's "backbone" from Provincetown to the canal, "regardless of what trees would have to be cut down or private property taken."[143]

Always, when progress seems to be moving in leaps and bounds, someone is turning back. A month after the bridges opened, Police Chief "Gunboat" Eldredge and his son "Gunny" went Aboriginal on the uninhabited tip of Morris Island for a week. A reporter from the *Boston Post* followed every move. Newspaper photos show the pair clad in bathing trunks and moccasins as they lived off the land, foraging for food, fishing and killing animals with a bow and arrow. One evening, it took the chief two full hours to kindle a fire.

From left, Joseph Nickerson Sr., Sarah Nickerson Ragan, Philip Nickerson, Ida Nickerson, Grace Dieghorn and Don Ragan enjoy a picnic at their North Beach Camp, circa 1936. *Photo courtesy of the Joseph A. Nickerson Jr. Collection.*

A Death and a Triumph

On August 3, 1936, Heman Andrew Harding died. Born in 1871, Harding was sixty-five. He had been in poor health for several years, suffering from diabetes and chronic myocarditis, referring cryptically in letters to "my old trouble." On July 31, a duodenal ulcer ruptured, and Harding died three days later at Cape Cod Hospital. "To Mother and me his loss is, of course, irreparable for we were utterly dependent upon him," his daughter Virginia wrote in a letter two months after his death.

As befit a man who lived so much of his life in the public eye, condolence letters poured in from a number of eminent lawyers and jurists. "I know of no other who will be so greatly missed in all affairs of town and state," one wrote. Another called him "an oracle among our townspeople." Yet a Mrs. Hoppins of Greenfield, New Hampshire, recalled a more intimate moment when Virginia ran her fingers up and down the portly Heman's vest and said, "Little tight Dad." Mrs. Hoppins added, "He slipped his arm around her so proudly." Joseph Lincoln wrote that he and Mrs. Lincoln "both knew and respected him as a good man and a leading citizen of Chatham."[144]

Chatham flags flew at half mast, and business was suspended in tribute to Harding. More than two hundred mourners trudged through a heavy rainstorm to attend Harding's funeral at his Main Street home. Among the six pallbearers was Edwin H. Kidder. Heman Harding, whose early vision of Chatham as a destination for tourists did so much to shape the town, was buried with Masonic rites.[145]

A few months later, Hannah Hammond touchingly sent Edith Harding a photograph of Harding as a small boy. "Heman looked like his mother," she wrote. "She had beautiful dark blue eyes and dark hair. He was her only child and she thought so much of him."

A year after Harding died, the town's park commissioners spoke about the popularity of the lighthouse park that Harding had conceived more than twenty years earlier, back in 1916. And as usual, popularity brought problems—namely, the surface of the road needed to be re-oiled in both fall and spring to keep it in shape. "There is no place in town that has the abuse this does. The town received income enough from the optical machines at the Chatham Light in the past season to help make some of these improvements," noted the 1937 town annual report.

The Chatham Light was "a landmark, a beacon for the travelers of the sea, and a guide to sailors," crowed the *Cape Cod Colonial*.[146] During the two-month season in 1936, over fifteen hundred people had toured the lighthouse. They came from almost every state, and even from as far as the west coast of

Africa. Many had never seen a light and were full of foolish questions such as "Is that a lighthouse?"

People, people. What to do with all these people?[147] As the town meeting loomed, an article came out in the *Monitor* on January 14, 1937, under the headline "Which Way Chatham?" Speaking of the need for planning—something that many Cape towns were looking at—the article writer, identified by the initials E.B.K., asked:

> *What kind of people do we want in our town as residents? Shall we let overnight cabins, clam restaurants and trailer camps drive out to other Cape towns the present substantial and future desirable citizens to towns nearby who with an eye to their future will welcome them?*

At the same time, Alice Guild noted, William H. Balfour was clearing his Main Street land, an old Eldredge property, of trees and the old barn. "We regret the loss of the big tree with so few shade trees on the street." Townspeople vigorously fought Balfour, who wanted to put up a filling station or, barring that, a "quick lunch place."

If a filling station wasn't bad enough, now murderers had come to town. On March 7, a trio of fishermen—Antone Elears Malhado, fifty, and the father/son duo of Lorenzo Scola, forty-seven, and his son, Salvatori Scola, twenty-four, of the North End of Boston—devoted an afternoon to drinking and fighting. Eventually, Malhado rowed out to his fishing boat, which was anchored twenty feet offshore—well within view of the Hawthorne Inn, should anyone have been watching from there off-season. Soon, a dory with the two Scolas slid up alongside. "There were words, blows of an oar, and blows with a knife. When it was over, Malhado lay on the bottom of the dory, a knife wound in his heart." Father and son Scola were soon arrested in Harwich Port. As Chief Eldredge noted in his annual police report, this was the first murder in Chatham since the police department was created in 1922.

"The chief reaction was one of dismay that it happened here," Alice Guild wrote in her column on March 11, 1937.

All along, as Chief Eldredge well knew, Chatham had had its seamy side. During the lean years of the Depression, breaking and entering and larceny had increased. The summer homes of the rich provided natural targets for those scrimping to get by day to day. An individual the papers called the "boy burglar" broke into a summer home and stole food and a few small articles. Another Chatham man broke into Smith's drugstore, looking for money. Throughout the 1920s, the chief had asked for more money to increase his

The 1915 Brick Block, Main Street, during a 1930s snowstorm. The commercial block, home to the post office and Quilty's, a popular spot to rendezvous for ice cream, had apartments on the second floor. *Photo courtesy of the Chatham, Massachusetts Historical Society.*

protection of the town. "The automobile has made it an easy matter for thieves to come into the country towns, do their work, and get away while the town sleeps," he wrote in the 1929 town annual report.

An incest case had garnered publicity in the early 1930s. And in 1933, Chief Eldredge and two of his deputies had disguised themselves as fishermen and joined in an illegal dice game, which they broke up. "The raid on the game followed complaints received by wives and mothers of the players," Chief Eldredge said.[148]

So much of the town's lore seemed to revolve around fishermen. Yet a 1937 survey of occupations on Cape Cod revealed that housekeeping was the most prominent occupation, with 37.8 percent of the population involved in it. This was followed by 13.7 percent engaged in unskilled labor. Only 2.6 percent were fishing.

On March 4, 1937, Harold Dunbar, now editing the *Cape Cod Beacon*, a "Magazine of Entertainment, Information and Humor," began a lengthy joke asserting that Cape Cod should secede. Dunbar received a reply from

President Franklin D. Roosevelt written by Roosevelt's assistant secretary. "The president was much amused by your letter—especially because he has a good many relatives on Cape Cod and would really hate to think of them as foreigners," H.H. McIntyre wrote.[149] Referring to himself as "the Sublime Coderator," Dunbar issued ukases such as "any person convicted of putting tomato in the clam chowder will be banished from the Republic. This is a civilized country."[150] (Chowder with tomato is, of course, known as Manhattan Clam Chowder.) He also wanted to change the name of the town to Port Fortune, in commemoration of de Champlain's arrival in 1606. Carol Wight, who had put up the monument to de Champlain across the street from his Stage Harbor home, shared the joke at a *Cape Cod Beacon* dinner in April 1937. Selectman Edwin Kidder rebutted that nothing could be done about the name change until "the town had studied it carefully from every angle."[151]

A week later, Guild noted that Wilfred Berube was erecting a fifty-by-sixty-five-foot airplane hangar at the airport that he was developing on seventy-two acres of land in West Chatham. From the early part of the '30s on, Berube, almost single-handedly, had been transforming the forest of scrub pines into open grassland suitable for a runway. By the mid-'30s, private planes had begun flying into Chatham Airport.[152]

Three men pose in front of a Nickerson Lumber Company truck. The lumber company's buildings were conveniently located by the old train yard, and in the 1930s the lumber company was the railroad's only freight customer. *Photo courtesy of the Chatham, Massachusetts Historical Society.*

In any event, the day of the Cape Cod train had come and gone. In July 1937, the New York, New Haven & Hartford Railroad Company closed down the eight-mile Chatham branch of the railroad after a study determined that the only use of the line was freight brought in to nearby Nickerson Lumber Company. Harold Dunbar, addressing the Chatham Woman's Club, begged not only that the town preserve the Old Mill but Chatham's 1887 train station as well. (And about twenty years later, Dunbar got his wish.)

The Hurricane of '38

By the summer of 1938, both Chatham's reliance on tourists for its economy and the Depression were well-established facts. Edna Matteson had been hired in 1937 to attend to the "comfort rooms" in the Chatham Board of Trade building on Chatham Bars Avenue. To the 1938 town annual report, Matteson contributed lively and well-thought-out remarks.

During the summer of 1938, Matteson said that she had expanded her duties far beyond policing the restroom's supply of towels and toilet paper. "In conjunction with this rest room, I took it upon myself to operate what was called the Chatham Information Bureau and I submit the following report," she wrote.

Matteson said that she began by presenting a "generous supply of all transportation literature for train, bus, express, boat and freight." She even "engineered" walking tours. She responded to 450 letters.

She operated as a job-clearing bureau too. "Many summer residents were helped out of difficult situations and many girls found work, some permanent positions."

Early in the fall of 1937, Mary Winslow, head of the new Monomoy Theatre, came to Matteson regarding her telephone. Matteson not only finagled the installation of the theatre's telephone, but she also had it listed in the summer directory. In the summer, Matteson placed twenty-five members of the troupe in lodging and arranged for their food and laundry to be taken care of.

In June, an author approached Matteson "for a spot where he would be quiet, for tenting space." Matteson settled him under the hill at the Chatham Coast Guard Station. There, the author contentedly lived through September, writing his (unnamed) novel.

Matteson goes on to chide the selectmen for the "inadequacy" of the "toilet system." Plagued with leaks and dampness, the toilet was "unpleasant." But beyond this, Matteson asks the selectman's permission to continue with her

The Chatham Board of Trade Building on Chatham Bars Avenue. The board was founded in 1919 "to promote the business and society interests of the inhabitants of the Town of Chatham." The building also offered a public restroom. *Photo courtesy of the Chatham, Massachusetts Historical Society.*

mission as an ambassadress to the town. (It appears that Matteson ultimately moved on.)

On September 21, 1938, the "Hurricane of '38," soon dubbed "the disaster of the century," struck New England. "First reports of the disaster came by radio, and among them it was said Cape Cod was isolated, even washed away," the *New Bedford Standard-Times* reported on September 24, 1938. "They built up the picture of horror." But the truth was that the area worst hit on Cape Cod was Woods Hole in Falmouth, and Chatham was mainly spared the destructive brunt of the storm.

The Winds of War

Early in January, the Cape Cod Chamber of Commerce selected a new field agent, Arthur R. Finley of Orleans. The chamber was to operate on a $25,000 annual budget to be used for answering inquiries, mailing literature, publishing three information booklets and placing advertisements in newspapers and magazines. A Boston advertising form, Badger and Browning, was to be brought in for the first time.

"I have spent over twenty years of my life in advertising and selling and know that Cape Cod has everything to offer," Finley said in a page-one article in the *Monitor* on January 1. "*But to enjoy the fullest results from what we have to sell, it must be advertised.*" (My italics.) In other words, a tourist destination doesn't just happen—it is created. Eventually, the group would print seventy-five thousand copies of a Cape Cod booklet with the title *Be Cool on Sea-Cooled Cape Cod: The Perfect Summer Vacationland*. Booklets would be distributed at the 1939 World's Fair in New York.

While the Cape was to be sold to off-Cape residents as an entire geographic package, back in Chatham the women's club was looking into a topic that might have been dear to Heman Harding—installing a restroom at Chatham Light. (Ultimately, the voters at the 1940 town meeting tabled the $1,500 request.)

As 1939 wore on, an awareness of the winds of war two thousand miles across the Atlantic entered into Alice's column. The town's registrar of voters had a new job—a house-to-house canvas to list all males ages eighteen and older and all females ages twenty-one and older. The reason for the discrepancy in ages is that the list of males might soon serve as a military registration list.

Two years earlier, a hotel in Germany had requested a shipment of Chatham oysters. The oysterman Ben Gould willingly sent over a barrel that was never acknowledged or paid for. "We think somebody ought to write to Mr. Hitler about that," Dunbar wrote in the *Cape Cod Beacon* in November 1937.

Meanwhile, Chatham was to get new telephones, doing away with the hand cranks then needed to call the operator. With the new system, a caller would simply pick up the telephone and the operator would say, "Number, please."

Alice Stallknecht gave a talk at the Ladies' Reading Club on Paraguay and brought a stash of leaves and twigs used by the South Americans to steep Yerba Maté tea. The reaction of the ladies of Chatham to this new tea was unfavorable.

A Mr. Gibson tore down the house he bought on Bridge Street and announced that he planned to build two houses "designed for summer rentals" on the lot, which "is a choice one as it commands a fine view of the Atlantic," Alice Guild reported on February 16, 1939.

Schools were closed in late February as an epidemic of the grippe raced through. Those old enough to remember 1918 must have let out sighs of relief every year when grippe season passed without a death toll.

A Friday noon picnic on the beach at the Chatham Beach and Tennis Club, just below the Chatham Light, 1942. The club, founded in 1927, gave the children of summer visitors a safe gathering place. *Photo courtesy of Ted Whittaker.*

The big elm in front of the Eldredge Library was to be cut down, as the heart of the tree was a mere cavity after a wind storm the previous fall.

Naval Reserve Unit 5 was meeting weekly and training in Chatham Port at the former site of the Naval Air Station—or what was left of it. For nearly twenty years, the abandoned site had been left to the elements and those scavenging for wood for their houses.

Miss Loomis Johnson told members of the garden club about her experiences feeding seagulls in the winter. "She told of their quick response to the noise of a spoon hitting the side of the food pan and other incidents." The Chatham Band gave its final performance of the season—an all-request concert. The band would probably move to the new Kate Gould Park the next year.

The population of the town in 1939 was 2,050, up 32 percent from the 1,564 residents of 1912. By now, real estate topped the $6.5 million mark, with nonresidents paying 52 percent of the tax burden.

Still, for all that life moved on as usual, the war across the waters intruded like a leitmotif. "Friends were relieved to hear from Miss Whitford Drake and her daughter, Miss Helen Drake, that they would arrive in Boston on Sunday. They have been traveling in Europe this summer," Guild noted.

Later Guild added, "The establishment of a permanent air base off our coast will give us more of a feeling of protection in our little villages. We understand the plans will guard our neutrality." Before Thanksgiving, those

The illustrator Harold Brett painted his friend, collaborator and fishing partner Joseph C. Lincoln (1870–1944). The painting now hangs in the Chatham Historical Society's Lincoln Room. *Photo by the author from a painting at the Chatham, Massachusetts Historical Society.*

attending a service at the Congregational church took up a special offering to help the "thousands of homeless refugees in war-stricken areas" in Europe.

"Have you noticed," Alice Guild wrote in her last column of 1939, "the beautiful simplicity of the lighted Madonna window in the Methodist church? It seems to give the whole town a spirit of reverence." She is glad that the town isn't under blackout restrictions that would prohibit Christmas lights.

Harold Dunbar and Joseph Lincoln would be too old to serve in World War II. In 1941, Dunbar would take a new wife, F. Gertrude Bower Buck, who was a child of seven on the day Harold married Brownie in 1913. "Our older Cape Cod is disappearing, and a neat, up-to-date summer-resort taking its place," Dunbar wrote in a 1940 letter to a woman who bought one of his paintings. Dunbar would die twelve years after his second wedding, of a sudden heart attack. He is buried at Seaside Cemetery in a single grave now overrun by a shrub.

Lincoln, too, would die of a heart attack in 1944 in a hotel in Winter Park, Florida. His ashes are buried at a family plot in Union Cemetery.

In the 1940s, Alice Stallknecht would paint a third large-scale mural, *Every Man to His Trade*, and once again Slim Hutchings, older now by more than a decade, perhaps just a bit less lanky, a bit more careworn, would pose as Christ—Christ the carpenter. When the two earlier murals were removed from the church, Alice bought an abandoned freight building sitting at the now-defunct Chatham Station, transported the building to her property and hung the original two murals with the third. During her lifetime Alice, although famous, only sold three or four paintings.

Alice lived to see how successful the selling of Chatham ultimately was. She died in 1973 at the age of ninety-three.

NOTES

Introduction

1. Thoreau, *Cape Cod*, 14.
2. Sargent, *Handbook*, 571.
3. J. Lincoln, *Cape Cod Yesterdays*, xiii.
4. Conforti, *Imagining New England*, 263.
5. Brown, *Inventing New England*, 205.
6. Thompson, *History*, 377.
7. F. Lincoln, *Joseph C. Lincoln Reader*, introduction.
8. Moore, "Joseph C. Lincoln's Presentation."
9. Conversation with Chatham artist Amy Dare Middleton, January 2009.

The End of Ragtime

10. Unpublished correspondence of August 1916, between Heman Andrew Harding and the Honorable Joseph Walsh, Chatham Historical Society.
11. Brown, *Inventing New England,* 202 ff.
12. Personal and legal documents of Heman A. Harding are stored in thirty-three boxes at the Chatham Historical Society. The papers, divided into the "Heman Harding Papers, 1920–1936" and the "Virginia Harding McGrath Papers, 1920–1936" were given to the society by the estate of McGrath and offer a vivid snapshot of Chatham from the late nineteenth century through the middle of the twentieth century.
13. Smith, *History of Chatham*, iv.
14. Unpublished tribute to Smith by Heman A. Harding, probably written after Smith's death on April 12, 1932. In the Smith family file, Chatham Historical Society.

15. Unpublished material in the Smith family file, Chatham Historical Society.
16. *Report of the Town Officers*, 1911.
17. This and all subsequent information on the bicentennial, unless noted, comes from *The Two Hundredth Anniversary of the Incorporation of the Town of Chatham, Massachusetts*, 1912.
18. Nickerson, *Days to Remember*, 237. No student of Chatham's history should miss this chatty, anecdotal account of life by a Chatham native born in 1901.
19. See the Centers for Disease Control website for an excellent discussion of smallpox: http://emergency.cdc.gov/agent/smallpox/overview/disease-facts.asp.
20. *Report of the Town Officers*, 1912.
21. Ibid., 1914.
22. In "Joseph C. Lincoln's Presentation of Cape Cod," Moore describes Chelsea as "urban, immigrant, industrial," highlighting that Lincoln was early on acquainted with towns unlike his native Cape Cod.
23. F. Lincoln, *Joseph C. Lincoln Reader*, introduction.
24. Ibid.
25. Unpublished correspondence between Alice Richards Fuller and her brother, Will, February 15, 1899, Chatham Historical Society.
26. Nickerson, *Days to Remember*, 230.
27. Stallknecht, *Something of My Past*.
28. Ibid.
29. *Report of the Town Officers*, 1913.
30. Unpublished letter from Heman A. Harding to H. Fisher Eldredge, January 1, 1914, Chatham Historical Society.
31. *Chatham's Old Houses*, Book III, 4.
32. Nickerson, *Days to Remember*, 270.
33. Ibid., 231.
34. Alice Smith oral interview, 1950s, Chatham Historical Society.
35. A summer resident later recalled his 1911 visit to the Mattaquason: "In each room stapled to the window frame and coiled beneath the window was a knotted rope with an instruction card saying in case of fire 'Throw out and descend to the ground.'" Undated newspaper, Chatham Historical Commission archives.
36. Chatham Historical Society.
37. Undated newspaper, Chatham Historical Society.
38. *Report of the Town Officers*, 1917.

39. Unpublished records of the Ladies' Reading Club, Chatham Historical Society.
40. The extensive archives of the Chatham Woman's Club are in the Chatham Historical Society.
41. This and the following material on Heman A. Harding's role in establishing the Marconi Company in Chatham, 1914–15, are to be found at the Chatham Historical Society.
42. Buckley, *Wings Over Cape Cod*, 48.
43. Ibid., 148.
44. *Chatham Monitor*, July 9, 1918.
45. Wight dedicated the 1918 play to "the Chatham Boys and Girls and Chatham Men and Women who have collaborated in our local plays for the past few years."
46. Barry, *The Great Influenza*, 169.
47. Ibid., 224.
48. Nickerson, *Days to Remember*, 244.
49. *Chatham Monitor*, October 8, 1918.
50. *Report of the Town Officers*, 1919.
51. Unpublished material on the Chatham Board of Trade, founded June 27, 1919, Chatham Historical Society.

The Jazz Age

52. *Cape Cod Beacon*, late July 1937, 24.
53. Unless otherwise noted, information on Harold Dunbar's divorce comes from the papers of Heman A. Harding at the Chatham Historical Society.
54. *Hyannis Patriot*, July 17, 1924.
55. "They called her the Gloria Vanderbilt of Chatham because she was so wealthy." Conversations with Isabel Lamberg, February 2007 and November 2008. Lamberg, born in 1926, spent childhood summers from 1936 on with her three aunts, the Stones, in the Main Street house next door to the one Harold Dunbar rented from Almena Kent and, later, from Josephine Atkins. Lamberg knew the "very abrupt" Miss Atkins and studied art in Dunbar's Chatham Summer School of Art. "They were the odd couple," Lamberg says of the flamboyant Dunbar and proper Atkins. "But they got along so well."
56. *Cape Cod Beacon*, late July, 1937, 30-31. In February 1937 Dunbar and partners decided to turn a weekly newspaper, the *Provincetown Beacon*,

which was first published in 1890, into a fortnightly magazine. The new editorial offices were in Yarmouthport. The publication schedule was haphazard at best at a price of $1.50 for twelve issues and $2.00 for eighteen.

57. Alexander, "Impact of Tourism," 320–26.
58. J. Lincoln, *Shavings*, 4.
59. *New Bedford Standard-Times*, September 6, 1931.
60. Ibid.
61. Unpublished documents, letters and photographs of Edwards posing with his customers are in the Chatham Historical Society.
62. *New Bedford Standard-Times*, September 6, 1931.
63. *New York Times*, undated clipping, Chatham Historical Society.
64. Unpublished documents concerning the church's 200th anniversary celebration are in the archives of the First Congregational Church of Chatham.
65. Historical records in the archives of the First Congregational Church of Chatham.
66. *Cape Cod Voice*, July 31, 2003.
67. Thompson, *History*, Vol. III, 275.
68. *Cape Cod Beacon*, June 15, 1937, 29.
69. Nickerson, *Days to Remember*, 65.
70. Ibid., 166.
71. A conversation among "old-time residents" sponsored by the Chatham Historical Society in June 1979. Unpublished transcript in the Chatham Historical Commission archives.
72. Henderson, *A Short History of Transportation in Chatham.*
73. Nutting, *Massachusetts Beautiful*, 41.
74. Ibid., 38.
75. Ibid., 17.
76. Conversation with Shirley Sabin of the Nauset Light Preservation Society, January 2009.
77. *Cape Cod Colonial*, February 8, 1937.
78. Carol Wight, "William Nickerson In Memoriam," *Chatham Monitor*, September 18, 1924.
79. Unpublished paper on the Old Atwood House, Chatham Historical Society.
80. Ibid.
81. Ibid.
82. Ibid.
83. *Cape Cod Beacon*, May 1937, 10.

84. Greene, "History of Development."
85. Nickerson, *Days to Remember*, 11.
86. Much of the information on the early history of Eastward, Ho! comes from Virginia Doherty's excellent book *The Story of Eastward, Ho! Country Club, Chatham, Massachusetts*, privately printed.
87. Faught, *Falmouth, Massachusetts*.
88. Unpublished letter from Heman Andrew Harding probably dating to 1923, Chatham Historical Society.
89. Unpublished letter, Chatham Historical Society.
90. Jonas, *That Which Brought Us Hither*, 5.
91. Louchheim, *My Crowd*, 86.
92. Hotel and inn brochures at the Chatham Historical Society.
93. *Cape Cod Chronicle*, September 9, 1982.
94. Cather, *Not Under Forty*, prefatory note.
95. *Who's Who in Massachusetts*, 243.
96. Material on the divorce comes from the legal files of Heman A. Harding, Chatham Historical Society.
97. Spaulding, *Intimate Incidents*, 16.
98. Letter from Fred L. Whalen to "Tom," printed in the *Chatham Monitor*, August 19, 1926.
99. Unpublished material at the Chatham Historical Society.

Brother, Can You Spare a Dime?

100. Most biographical information about Alice Stallknecht Wight comes from *Something of My Past*, an unpublished memoir.
101. Among the "Ten Commandments for Cape Cod" are the following rules: "Treat the Visitor Fairly. The overcharged visitor not only never returns; he warns everyone else to stay away" and "Remember that the Visitor Is Both Guest and Customer."
102. Nickerson, *Days to Remember*, 57.
103. Information on Carol Wight's career both as a student and as a professor of classics at Johns Hopkins University is at the Chatham Historical Society.
104. *Cape Cod Chronicle*, May 23, 1991.
105. *New York Times*, Letter to the Editor, 1939.
106. Unpublished letter and water company booklet, Chatham Historical Society.
107. Unpublished correspondence between Joseph C. Lincoln and Heman A. Harding, Chatham Historical Society.

108. *Cape Cod Beacon*, March 1937.
109. Unpublished papers in the Chatham Historical Society.
110. Conversation, December 2008. In 2005, Ted Whittaker coauthored, with his childhood friend the artist John Hutchinson, an illustrated book called *Beach Wagons in Chatham*. "Woodies," as they were called, were wooden-sided automobiles rigged out with underinflated, oversized balloon tires for easy driving through the beach sands. Their book poignantly describes the lost days of woodies on Monomoy.
111. Undated newspaper clipping, Chatham Historical Society.
112. *Herald Tribune*, August 4, 1932.
113. Ibid.
114. *Time Magazine*, August 15, 1932. "Critics [of Stallknecht] also recalled that modernized divinities are nothing new; Jacob Epstein's Christ was much discussed for his negroid appearance," the article notes.
115. See Ingrid A. Steffensen and Patricia Likos Ricci's excellent paper "Alice Stallknecht: Every Woman to Her Trade." The authors examine the arc of Stallknecht's painting career within the context of her roles as daughter, wife and mother.
116. For an interesting discussion of murals of the 1930s and 1940s see Kammen, *Visual Shock*, 119–48.
117. Unpublished church history and notes in the archives of the First Congregational Church of Chatham.
118. Unpublished sermon given by Franklin P. Cole on the occasion of the 250th anniversary of the First Congregational Church of Chatham, June 7, 1970.
119. Essay by Edward S. Cook Jr. in *History and Humor*, 18.
120. *New Bedford Sunday Standard-Times*, August 7, 1932.
121. Unpublished letter from Franklin P. Cole to L. Sidney Atwood, June 29, 1932, archives of the First Congregational Church of Chatham.
122. Cole rebutted the Reverend Carl A. Seaward of Swampscott in an undated newspaper clipping in the Chatham Historical Society.
123. Unpublished notes on Cole's ministry are in the archives of the First Congregational Church of Chatham.
124. *Reports of the Town Officers*, 1937.
125. Much of the information on Buck comes from an unpublished, undated, ninety-page typed plea for a commutation of his sentence that Kenneth Earle Buck wrote from state prison. At the Chatham Historical Society.
126. *Chatham Monitor*, May 4, 1933.
127. Ibid., May 11, 1933.

128. Unpublished documents, Chatham Historical Society.
129. Website of the Army Corps of Engineers.
130. *Cape Cod Beacon*, mid-August 1937, 35. Dunbar had an attitude to alcohol that might serve as a reminder as to why Prohibition came to be in the first place. "We never drive so well or so cautiously as when we are drunk, and we are convinced that if everybody would keep mildly drunk most of the time, the world would be a much more agreeable place," he wrote in the *Cape Cod Beacon*, March 1938, 2.
131. J. Lincoln, *Cape Cod Yesterdays*, 5.
132. *New Bedford Standard-Times*, July 24, 1935.
133. Conversation with Reggie Nickerson, October 2008. Nickerson is pictured in Stallknecht's third mural, *Every Man to His Trade*, as an eighteen-year-old Sea Scout. Nickerson met Stallknecht when he was helping to rescue boats that had strayed inland next to her house during the hurricane of 1944.
134. Unpublished letter from Reverend Thorp to Alice Stallknecht Wight, September 27, 1935; archives of the First Congregational Church of Chatham.
135. *Cape Cod Beacon*, April 1937, 13. Ariel took his name from the blithe spirit who did the bidding of Prospero in Shakespeare's *The Tempest*, Dunbar explained in his *Beacon* of mid-August 1937. It is most likely that Ariel, who drew a series of caricatures for the *Beacon*, was one of Dunbar's many aliases.
136. Unpublished church history in the archives of the First Congregational Church of Chatham.
137. Unpublished letter from Maud B. Church to Arthur Edwards, September 13, 1933, Chatham Historical Society.
138. Unpublished letter to Arthur Edwards's daughter, September 6, 1938, from the New York, New Haven & Hartford Railroad Company, Chatham Historical Society.
139. *Chatham's Old Houses*, Book V, 24.
140. *Cape Cod Beacon*, June 1, 1937, 8.
141. *Cape Cod Beacon*, mid-August, 1937, 3. The director of one play, *Caprice*, received an anonymous letter from a theatre-goer in Wellfleet. "Evidently this Dunbar who played the part of the Doctor, was a local son. I suppose you picked him in order to mollify the local hicks. But why should I pay my good money to see anything like that?"
142. See the U.S. Army Corps of Engineers website for a history of the building of the bridges: www.nae.usace.army.mil/recreati/ccc/education/canalbridges.htm.

143. *Chatham Monitor*, September 12, 1935.
144. The unpublished letters of condolence written to Edith and Virginia Harding upon Heman Harding's death make poignant reading. They are located at the Chatham Historical Society.
145. *New Bedford Standard-Times*, undated clipping, Chatham Historical Society.
146. *Cape Cod Colonial*, February 8, 1937.
147. By the end of 1937, Harold Dunbar was preaching against advertising the Cape because of the "hordes of cheap people who came and went all summer, crowding the beaches, jamming the streets of our villages, trespassing on private property, damaging boats, and making themselves a general nuisance." Who benefitted? Those who owned hotdog stands, trailer camps and cheap souvenir shops. A good thing had gone too far. *Cape Cod Beacon*, November 1937, 2.
148. *New Bedford Standard-Times*, 1949, article upon retirement of Eldredge.
149. *Cape Codder*, November 23, 1950.
150. *Cape Cod Beacon*, June 15, 1937, 5.
151. Undated newspaper clipping with the headline "Society to Change Chatham's Name to Port Fortune Stirs Controversy," Chatham Historical Society.
152. Information on Berube and the building of the Chatham Airport comes from Whittier, *Mon Reve: My Dream*.

BIBLIOGRAPHY

Books and Articles on Chatham and Cape Cod

Alexander, Lewis M. "The Impact of Tourism on the Economy of Cape Cod, Massachusetts." *Economic Geography* 29 (1953): 320–26.

Barr, Nancy, with illustrations by Kassie Foss. *A Sense of Place by the Sea: The Legacy of Chatham's Homes*. Chatham, MA: Town of Chatham, 2007.

Bassett, Sara Ware. *Twin Lights*. New York: A.L. Burt, 1932.

Bell, Arthur W. *Cape Cod Color*. Boston: Houghton Mifflin Company, 1931.

Buckley, Joseph. *Wings Over Cape Cod: Chatham Naval Air Station 1917–1922*. Orleans, MA: Lower Cape Publishing, 2000.

Cape Cod Beacon, March 1937; April 1937; May 1937; June 1, 1937; June 15, 1937; late July 1937; mid-August 1937; November 1937; and March 1938.

Carlisle, Robert D.B. *Weathering a Century of Change: Chatham, Cape Cod: The Story of a Seaside Village 1900–2000*. Chatham, MA: Chatham Historical Society, 2000. [A comprehensive look at major events in Chatham during the twentieth century.]

Chatham's Old Houses. Books I to VI. Chatham, MA: Chatham Historical Society, 1962–67.

Doherty, Virginia. *The Story of Eastward, Ho! Country Club, Chatham, Massachusetts*. N.p., n.d.

Faught, Millard C. *Falmouth, Massachusetts: Problems of a Resort Community*. New York: Columbia University Press, 1945.

Greene, H.U. "History of Development: Cape and Vineyard Electric Company, 1923–1933." Unpublished paper, n.d.

Henderson, Eleanor. *A Short History of Transportation in Chatham*. N.p., n.d.

Hutchinson, John, and Ted Whittaker. *Beach Wagons in Chatham*. N.p.: 2005.

Ivanoff, Josephine Buck. *Pieces of Old Cape Cod*. N.p.: 1985.

Jonas, Connie K. *That Which Brought Us Hither: The History of Harding Shores, The Reminiscences of the residents of a spit of sand on Cape Cod in West Chatham, Massachusetts*. 2nd edition. N.p.: 2005.

Kittredge, Henry C. *Cape Cod: Its People and Their History*. 2nd edition. Boston: Houghton Mifflin Company, 1968.

Lincoln, Freeman, ed. *The Joseph C. Lincoln Reader*. New York: Appleton-Century-Crofts, 1959.

Lincoln, Joseph C. *Cape Cod Yesterdays*. New York: Blue Ribbon Books, 1935.

———. *Shavings, a Novel*. New York: D. Appleton and Company, 1918.

Nickerson, Joshua Atkins, II. *Days to Remember: A Chatham Native Recalls Life on Cape Cod Since the Turn of the Century*. Chatham, MA: Chatham Historical Society, 1988.

Pacun, Carol, and Norman Pacun. *The History of the Chatham Beach and Tennis Club, 1927–1992*. N.p., n.d.

Picturing Chatham. Chatham, MA: Chatham Historical Society, 2001.

Reports of the Town Officers of the Town of Chatham. Chatham, MA: Chatham Monitor Print, published annually.

Rex, Percy Fielitz. *The Prolific Pencil: A Biography of Joseph Crosby Lincoln, Litt.D.* Taunton, MA: William S. Sullwold Publishing, Inc., 1980.

Smith, William C. *A History of Chatham Massachusetts*. Chatham, MA: Chatham Historical Society, 1971.

Tarbell, Arthur Wilson. *Cape Cod Ahoy! A Travel Book for the Summer Visitor*. Boston: Little, Brown and Company, 1935.

———. *I Retire to Cape Cod*. New York: Stephen Daye, Inc., 1944.

Thoreau, Henry David. *Cape Cod*. New York: Bramhall House, 1951.

The Two Hundredth Anniversary of the Incorporation of the Town of Chatham, Massachusetts. Chatham, MA: Town of Chatham, 1912.

Other Helpful Sources

Allen, Frederick Lewis. *Only Yesterday: An Informal History of the 1920s*. New York: Harper & Row, 1931.

Barry, John M. *The Great Influenza: The Epic Story of the Deadliest Plague in History*. New York: Viking, 2004.

Brown, Dona. *Inventing New England: Regional Tourism in the Nineteenth Century*. Washington, D.C.: Smithsonian Press, 1995.

Cather, Willa. *Not Under Forty*. New York: A.A. Knopf, 1936.

Conforti, Joseph A. *Imagining New England: Explorations of Regional Identity From The Pilgrims to the Mid-Twentieth Century*. Chapel Hill: University of North Carolina Press, 2001.

D'Entremont, Jeremy. *The Lighthouse Handbook New England*. Kennebunkport, ME: Cider Mill Press Book Publishers, 2008.

Federal Writers' Project. *The WPA Guide to Massachusetts*. New York: Pantheon Books, 1983.

History and Humor: The Folk Art Figures of Franklin P. Cole. Portland, ME.: Portland Museum of Art, 2000.

Kammen, Michael. *Visual Shock: A History of Art Controversies in American Culture*. New York: Vintage Books, 2007.

Kolata, Gina. *Flu: The Story of the Great Influenza Pandemic of 1918 and the Search for the Virus that Caused It*. New York: Farrar, Straus and Giroux, 1999.

Kyvig, David E. *Daily Life in the United States, 1920–1940: How Americans Lived Through the "Roaring Twenties" and the Great Depression*. Chicago: Ivan R. Dee, 2002.

Louchheim, Mary. *My Crowd*. N.p.: 2003.

McCutcheon, Marc. *The Writer's Guide to Everyday Life from Prohibition through World War II*. Cincinnati, OH: Writer's Digest Books, 1995.

Moore, William D. "Joseph C. Lincoln's Presentation of Cape Cod." Paper given at the Joseph Crosby Lincoln Conference at the Chatham Historical Society, 2004.

Nutting, Wallace. *Massachusetts Beautiful*. New York: Bonanza Books, 1923.

Ricci, Patricia Likos. "Alice Stallknecht (1880–1973), Cape Cod Regionalist." Paper given at the conference Beneath the Surface: The Art of Alice Stallknecht at the Chatham Historical Society, 2003.

Sargent, Porter E. *A Handbook of New England*. Boston: Porter E. Sargent, 1916.

Spaulding, Huldah Wellington. *Intimate Incidents of an Antique Shop*. Hyannis, MA: self-published, 1932.

Stallknecht, Alice. *Something of My Past*. Unpublished memoir, n.d.

Steffensen, Ingrid A., and Patricia Likos Ricci. "Alice Stallknecht: Every Woman to Her Trade." *Woman's Art Journal* 26, no. 2: 14–18.

Thompson, Elroy S. *History of Plymouth, Norfolk and Barnstable Counties, Massachusetts*. Vol. III. New York: Lewis Historical Publishing Company, Inc., 1928.

Whittier, Bob. *Mon Reve: My Dream, The Story of Wilfred J. Berube and His Airport at Chatham on Cape Cod*. Duxbury, MA: Aviation Book Division, 1992.

Who's Who in Massachusetts. Vol. I, *1940–1941*. Boston: Larkin, Roosevelt & Larkin, Ltd., 1940.

ABOUT THE AUTHOR

Debra Lawless is a freelance writer living in Chatham. She earned a BA in history and classics at Stanford University and an MS in journalism at Boston University. A native of Providence, Rhode Island, she has worked for several newspapers and as a political press secretary. Currently, she writes for the *Cape Cod Chronicle*, specializing in books and authors. She is interested in historic preservation and the visual arts and is a member of the Chatham Historical Society, where Alice Stallknecht's murals are now on display.